# THE FRAGMENTED LIFE OF DON JACOBO LERNER

# THE FRAGMENTED LIFE OF DON JACOBO LERNER

by Isaac Goldemberg

*translated from the Spanish by*
*Robert S. Picciotto*

SIDGWICK & JACKSON
LONDON

*The characters and events in this
novel are wholly fictional and
any resemblance to actual
persons is coincidental.*

First published in Great Britain in 1978
by Sidgwick and Jackson Limited.

Originally published in the U.S.A. in 1976
by Persea Books Inc.

Printed in the United States of America
Designed by Bernard Schleifer

*To Mona, David and Dina*

*The publisher wishes to thank the Center for Inter-American Relations for their generosity and cooperation in helping to make this translation possible.*

# I

THE NIGHT before he died, Jacobo Lerner thought of the mild catastrophes that would be occasioned by his passing. He imagined his sister-in-law living on, unable to love anyone else. His brother Moisés he imagined bankrupt, abandoned by his son, asking for help from friends. His mistress, doña Juana Paredes Ulloa, he imagined reviled by everyone because she had not known how to squeeze money out of him in payment for her love. He imagined his sister-in-law's sister, Miriam Abramowitz, in deep repentance because she had not married him, who was now dead and buried. His son, Efraín, he imagined at the task of reconstructing his father from what was said by others. And Efraín's mother, who continued to live in the village where Lerner had met her, he imagined a victim of her father's insults for not having married the Jew while it was still possible.

He thought, too, almost melancholically, that his last will and testament would not have any effect whatever on whether or not these things came to pass.

The frayed yarmulke from the days of his childhood in Staraya Ushitza, he left to Moisés. To doña Juana Paredes he left the Louis XVI bed (with the pink coverlet that she herself had made) on which for the last five years they had frolicked like adolescents, three times a week. To Miriam he left an invitation in black gothic script and gold filigree for the wedding that never took place. To Efraín he left a small sum of money obtained through fourteen years of work and privations, for the day when he became twenty-one. To his sister-in-law he left the complete works of Heine, in German, with a dedication in Yiddish on the flyleaf written three years before, when he thought of giving her the book for her birthday.

Jacobo Lerner also remembered that the last time he saw his old friend León Mitrani was in 1925, on the day that Jacobo left for Lima, nine years before Mitrani died, victim of carelessness on the part of the village druggist, who instead of selling him the fifty milligrams of bicarbonate of soda prescribed by Doctor Meneses, sold him the same quantity of stain remover. He imagined Mitrani in the half-darkness of the grocery store, sitting placidly in the same rocking chair, behind the same counter where he had spent the last years of his life, bounded by ramshackle half-empty shelves and the ceiling on which spiders had woven their complicated structures, imperfect tetrahedrons. It was Samuel Edelman who had told him Mitrani died in the first hours of the morning, invoking the name of Jacobo Lerner between spasms and memories of his childhood in Staraya Ushitza.

"If you come to Chepén, you will be rich in a very short time," Mitrani had assured him in one of his letters. And Jacobo had found him prematurely old, dragging a lame leg, which Mitrani explained was the result of a kick by the mule used by Serafín, the water-seller, in 1922. It was the middle of winter when Jacobo Lerner arrived in Chepén with a suitcase full of trinkets on his shoulder, three years after his friend. He realized how much Mitrani had changed since the last time they had seen each other aboard the SS *Bremen* in Hamburg. Besides the lameness that Jacobo found intimidating because the man dragging his leg was the same age as he, Mitrani seemed to be weighed down by heavy premonitions of things to come.

One afternoon, as they sat in the café, Mitrani told Jacobo it would not be long before the northern part of the country would be swept by a violent pogrom. Samuel Edelman, a salesman who came to town every other month to keep Mitrani supplied with merchandise and who brought all the news, both national and foreign, that did not reach Chepén, had reported that in Trujillo, a city about one hundred kilometers away, the army had been preparing for months to move against the Jews who had settled between Chimbote and Tumbes. The Jewish community of Lima had already been liquidated, and the government had decreed that Jews living in the provinces should suffer the same fate as soon as possible.

According to Mitrani, that was what Edelman, who was now fleeing toward the jungle where he was sure he would not be found, had communicated to him. It is quite possible that if Jacobo Lerner had not been at least partly successful in ridding him of these delusions, Mitrani would have carried out his own planned flight to Iquitos and left behind the woman with whom he had been living since a month after his arrival in the town. And even when he remained, Mitrani never completely stopped being afraid that there would be a pogrom in Chepén. The murder of his uncle by the Czarist soldiers, in 1911, had been burned into his brain and remained there no matter what happened to him.

# ON JEWS IN PERU

(Exclusive for *Jewish Soul*)

We have lately seen a commercial and industrial guide to Loreto, published in 1916, and were very surprised to discover the great number of Jewish establishments that exist in Iquitos.

In the aforementioned guide we found an article entitled "The Amazon River Was Navigated by Hebrews and Phoenicians," that begins thus:

"Onfroy de Toron, in his work, *Earliest Navigation of the Ocean: Voyages of King Solomon's Ships to the Amazon,* proves that Hebrews and Phoenicians took their ships up the Amazon River which they named the Solomon, after the great King."

MAURICIO GLEIZER

Iquitos, January, 1923

# THE WANDERING JEW

(Exclusive for *Jewish Soul*)

Those who have seen the Wandering Jew in his nocturnal walks say that he is a man over one hundred years old and at least seven feet tall. He is dressed in a black frock-coat and, at the end of a crook, he carries a lamp whose flame is eternal. The detail that most impresses those who have met the apparition, however, is the horrifying sound of his iron spurs.

Whenever he is seen, epidemics or droughts follow shortly after.

An anonymous chronicler recorded the following event, witnessed by the inhabitants of Huancavelica at the turn of the century:

"On that day, it became suddenly dark and then a mysterious light, a kind of Aurora Borealis, illuminated the village so that the terrified townspeople could see how their huts were lifted high in the air, whirling like feathers along with their chickens, ducks, and sheep. The earth shook and, finally, they saw the Wandering Jew rise on a ball of fire that flew into the distance until all that was left of his presence was a glow behind the hills."

FRAY FERNANDO,
Lay Brother of the Convent
of La Merced

# Chronicles: 1923

President Augusto B. Leguía tries to dedicate the Republic to the Sacred Heart of Jesus. Under the pressure of students and workers led by Víctor Raúl Haya de la Torre, he gives up his undertaking.

Reb Teodoro Schneider, talmudic scholar and renowned for his knowledge of the Cabala, is named rabbi of the Jewish community of Lima. Mr. Alfredo Kaufman, owner of "La Confianza" furniture store, is elected president of the Hebrew Union, while Mr. Simón Rapaport is now in charge of administering the Synagogue of Breña. As for the Jewish Cemetery of Bellavista, Eliezer Greenberg, brother-in-law of the recently deceased Rabbi Weinstein, is designated caretaker.

Messrs. Moisés Lerner and Daniel Abramowitz are married to the sisters Sara and Miriam Brener in a double ceremony. After a reception at the Hebrew Union attended by their many friends, they leave for their honeymoon in the resort of Paracas, where the couples spend a happy week by the seaside.

At the Central Hotel, facing the main square of Guadalupe, Samuel Edelman is lying in his room, reading the letter that a well-known Peruvian intellectual has sent to the editor of *Jewish Soul.*

Lima, May 22, 1923

My Distinguished Friend:

A few days ago, while reading issue #3 of your magazine with great pleasure, I came across a letter which referred to the task that you, the Jews, have undertaken in our country. Although many men of your race have contributed in great measure to the progress of the nation, I would like to state that there is one more contribution of great importance that Judaism could make to Peru.

I refer to the mixing of that restless race with our own Indian one, the issue of which would certainly be the ideal type of Andean man. We would then see combined the strength and physical toughness of the Indian with the mental agility and the dynamism of the Jew.

This would be the new man, that is to say, the Peruvian type, unmistakably itself.

I firmly believe that it is time for all Jews to abandon the Old World; the New World should be their field of action and their Promised Land. In America your people must look for the remains of that legend left by those who preceded you in colonial times.

I am, sir, your most obedient servant,

Dr. Jose Eugenio Miranda

Edelman smiles with satisfaction when he finishes reading the letter, thinking that Dr. Miranda is a man of undeniable intellectual gifts.


Mrs. Golda Bernstein, Mr. Manuel Gosovsky, Miss Pola Fishman and Mr. Nuhim Prioz have arrived from Europe. Messrs. Miguel and Marcos Lemor have left for Huancayo, while Mrs. Ana Metz has left for Huacho, don Jorge Kaplivsky for Panama, don Jacobo Lerner for Chepén, and Mrs. Sara Gutin for Chimbote.

# II

## *Efraín: Chepén, 1932*

I DON'T know why Grandfather stuffs himself while we're half-starved. I sure would like to eat that steak and fried eggs with the mound of rice on the side since I don't like soups and stews very much. True that sometimes Bertila takes me to doña Chepa's restaurant and then I really get my fill of dishes so good we don't even get them for Easter at home; Grandmother says it is because there is no money, but Grandfather has such a steak every day that Iris, Ricardo, and I drool. Doctor Meneses says Ricardo needs vitamins, or maybe he said it about me, I don't really remember. But don't sing that tune to Grandfather. The truth is, I don't like wine very much but I would buy myself an orange crush for lunch and another one for dinner, because then I would have two bottle tops a day, fourteen a week and sixty a month, and there would be no one in school with more bottle tops than me. I would even give a few to Ricardo if I felt like it, but I am not going to give them to him if he keeps on bothering me. Yesterday he hid my reading book from me and Miss Angelita screamed at me in front of everyone because I didn't know my lesson. But then all the money is gone, and Bertila says what are we going to do? Again chick-peas with the rice and not any butter at all, not even for breakfast, and I'm not going to have my bread with just sugar. I drink my chocolate not too hot, because if I burn my tongue I won't be able to speak again. Grandmother says Bertila spends all the money on crap instead of giving her enough to buy some chickens; then we would have fried eggs every morning, turned over so that the yolk is hard and mealy.

One of these days Grandfather is going to die and leave us the money in his strong-box and we're going to have to bury him wrapped up in his blanket. The only one who loves me, after all, is Aunt Francisca, even though she scolds me and makes me read the catechism every night before I go to sleep. I tell her if I die, bury me in a shoe box with my bottle tops, but her eyes light up bright and her chin shakes and she says that only pure souls go to heaven; God doesn't protect boys who don't behave and don't say their prayers at night and don't go to church on Sundays to be blessed by Father Chirinos. Aunt Francisca must be the only saint in the family because my other aunts are lost souls who don't even go to mass any more and they haven't confessed their sins for years. Aunt Irma ran away last year with a sergeant of the Republican Guard whose spurs jingled when he came to visit her on Sundays. Grandmother says that they live as lovers in Pacasmayo and that they are going to burn in the fires of hell. Beatriz and Zoila are younger than Bertila. They're gone the whole day and late at night they come home drunk, with their hair all messed up and their dresses like crinkly cellophane. Zoila is the prettiest of all my aunts. Last year she was the queen of the carnival and the druggist is in love with her. She was so pretty with her ribbon tied in a bow she looked like a Spanish lady, and Grandfather is very happy because the druggist has a lot of money and he says that he is a serious man. When the royal carriage went by the sidewalks were covered with red and white flowers and with confetti that people tossed from their balconies. Grandfather is always asking Zoila when she is going to get married, and telling her to watch herself, not to be like Bertila, who let herself be had, and look at her now. Once Zoila had a pink silk dress and a crown of shining pearls; she looked like a princess in one of the fairy tales that Iris tells me.

Aunt Francisca gets so mad she almost has a stroke every

time she sees Beatriz and Zoila go out all painted up "as if they were whores." She says they are staining the name of the Wilsons, who were recognized and respected by everyone when they lived in Cajamarca in their father's house, even if now they're not. I don't know whether I am a Wilson or an Alvarado. Grandfather says "they arrived to this land in the last century, respectable, industrious, decent people," and Grandmother says "we have no need to envy those bland, long, thin, English people." When I ask Aunt Francisca if Grandfather is my father, or whether it is Uncle Pedro, she answers that I have no father, that he died seven years ago, before I was born. She doesn't remember too well, she says, but it seems that his store burned up, and he died in the flames the same as if he had been in hell. I'm not going to die like my father because I am a good boy who goes to mass every Sunday, and I go to confession, and I collect images of saints. Father Chirinos promised to give me an image of our patron, Saint Sebastian, who died shot through by the arrows of barbarians who adored a different god than ours. But Jesus Christ is the only true god, and I have to believe in him, or I will die and be condemned for sure, like Matilde's son, who was born with two heads so that they didn't let him be buried in holy ground. They say they took him to some other village and buried him in a cardboard box, with his bottle tops. When I get the image of Saint Sebastian, the biggest one of all and in colors, I will have fifty-two, and I am going to put it on the wall above my bed. But I'm going to have to wait because Father Chirinos doesn't give it away just like that. You have to really earn it, being very good and learning all the prayers by heart, before he gives it to you, and for me it's very difficult because sometimes, like when I have to say the Our Father, I am thinking of other things, like my father, who is not in heaven but burning slowly in hell. Grandmother says that he was a heretic son-of-a-bitch who brought perdition to our house. *Blessed be thy name . . .* My name at home is Efraín, but in the street and at school they call me little Jacobo, though the teacher only knows me as the grandson of don Efraín Wilson or the son of Bertila who a few years back made a big mistake and believed a lot of lies. Bertila didn't leave the house for two years and even tried to kill herself like a fool one night when she went into the deepest part of the river without knowing how to swim. She was half-drowned when they pulled her out and screaming they should let her die because she was so ashamed and would never again set foot in the street. *Thy kingdom come; thy will be done in earth as it is in heaven* . . . how could she stand it, she said, now that everyone knew what had happened to her? That night Grandfather cursed the Jew, the whore that gave him birth, and all his ancestors. . . . And Grandmother, like a fury, blaming Grandfather, calling him a shitty old man. Where the hell was he when they were fucking his daughter? Where was she? She also blamed herself for having done nothing, as much of a procuress as the old man, even though she had known that nothing good could come from those Sunday visits. Francisca had already warned doña Jesús that Bertila was headed on the wrong track. What kind of example was that for her daughters, who were already grown enough for the devil to tickle their bodies and make their insides feel warm, with Bertila crying at night like Iris when she lost her little Chinese doll, not letting me sleep . . . *Forgive us our trespasses as we forgive those who trespass against us.* I hate to hear her speak of her misfortune because afterward I have horrible nightmares of a witch with a long nose and hair all over her face, and eyes like those of a snake, who fries me in boiling oil. All my screaming bounces off the walls of the house as if I were inside a deflated ball. Bertila can't hear. Bertila never hears, always minding her business locked up in her world. Sometimes it is very peaceful: stories from the Bible where everything is pretty, bicycle rides by the river, fig trees and acacias, white clouds and skies as blue as the cloak worn by the virgin in the church . . . *lead us not into temptation* . . . But some other times Bertila looks at me with bloodshot eyes and keeps staring at me while she curses practically everyone, and then I shiver all over and I am afraid even of going to sleep because I know I am going to dream that they chop my head off and that Father Chirinos throws me in the river so the crabs will eat me. Aunt Francisca says crabs are just like devils with steel claws and white sharp teeth to reach straight for the heart. I never call Bertila then, because I know that she never comes, and I try to hold onto a rock to save myself. But the rock is covered with thick slime that is very slippery, and the current sweeps me away while the rock stays behind laughing like a giant face that I do not recognize. It has a mask painted on, like the clowns that come to the village with the circus. Everything gets darker. I fall deeper and deeper in the well that is full of Jews who are also something like devils, with long, sharp tails they use like wasps against Jesus Christ, whom Father Chirinos says is the Savior of the world, Son of God, and Father of all Christians. I can see him whenever I want, because his hands and feet are nailed to the cross so he can't leave the church. Father Chirinos says the church is our house as well, but Bertila never comes with us on Sundays to see him. Aunt Francisca says it's because she has the devil in her body, and it is going to eat her up little by little, until only a shadow is left, and then not even that. So I have to go to mass by myself and not only that, when I told her that Father Chirinos had made me an altar boy, she started to laugh like crazy and said it was really the living end, she would like to see the Jew's face now, to find out what he thought of having an altar-boy son. I didn't know who she was talking about, whether it was about the devil or about Mr. Mitrani, who is the only Jew I know. But that lame old man could not possibly be my father, because I would die of fright and shame. Besides, Aunt Francisca has told me that I shouldn't even get close to him, because he grinds up little boys and bakes them into pies.

It's better if I don't think of these things, because when I do I get dizzy and shake, and I know I won't be able to sleep the whole night. I hope Ricardo doesn't sleep. I would like to ask him whether he knows if there are any other Jews in the village besides Mitrani. Mitrani is nothing more than a crazy old man who spends his Sundays preaching in the square in front of the church about the end of the world that is near. He says the river will flood the houses, that we will all drown, that the anger of God will fall on our heads like a sword, that no one in this village will be saved because we are all damned . . .

If the end of the world comes, perhaps I'll see my father . . .

and Father Chirinos gets so angry because more people are out in the square, listening to the rantings of Mitrani, than in church. I like to be inside, surrounded by those smiling and silent saints and the cherubs, round and rosy like Iris' doll. They watch very carefully. You can't stick your finger in your nose, or scratch where you itch, or pinch the legs of the daughters of Polo Miranda, even if they give themselves airs because their father has a lot of money and owns the mill at Santa Fe . . .

and Father Chirinos begins the mass. I like to kneel and raise my eyes to Christ on the cross who looks a little bit like Mr. Mitrani, with the same nose and the same long, wavy eyelashes. Of course it can't be true because Mitrani is a heretic, like my father was. I like to look at the Virgin, who protects us from all evil, even from the voice of Mr. Mitrani, who is still shouting outside the church. I have no father. My only father is Jesus Christ, who is in heaven with the Holy Family. My family is not holy. They are all a bunch of whores and procurers, except Aunt Francisca, who is a real saint.

Like when Bertila tells me not to wait for her at night, that she is going to visit Irma in Pacasmayo and won't be back until the next day, and Aunt Francisca has to take me to her house to sleep. She has some flowers in a vase on top of the dresser and they have a smell that goes deep inside my head. It makes me sleepy and makes me think of cemeteries. When the druggist's mother died, Zoila took me with her when she went to leave some red flowers on the grave. It makes me sleepy, lying on the bed with the lumpy mattress and the bedbugs that I feel crawling on my body.

Aunt Francisca wakes me up, in the middle of the night always, and drags me, dying of fear, to wash my fingers in the basin because they are all sticky. She says I am already grown and have to stop doing that. Only swinish men do that, she says, not good boys.

When I sleep with Iris, Iris says nothing. She comes closer to rub herself against me and she puts her hand between my legs. The next day she avoids looking at me, as if she were ashamed.

I guess I won't be able to talk to Ricardo until tomorrow, in school. I don't know whether I'm going to go. I didn't do my homework, and Miss Angelita said she's going to ask us questions about the Inca empire. It's a story all about a man called Manco Kapac, who is the father of all Peruvians, and comes out of Lake Titicaca with his wife, and that's all I remember. I think he might have something to do with the god of the sun and a rod of gold that was stuck in the hill as if by magic, but I don't really know because I haven't looked at the book. The book has nice pictures in color of men with beards riding horses. Those are the heroes who made the country. There's also a picture of the flag and another of the national seal. I remember a crown of laurel leaves, and a flame, and a very green tree, and against a red background a horn-of-plenty full of golden coins. I have to read that tomorrow. I'm going to do it instead of going fishing in the river with Ricardo.

I'm getting dizzy, but it's better if I don't say anything. It would only make Grandfather angry, like last night, at dinner, when I asked him again and Bertila gave me the usual answer: "You are the son of the rock." And Grandmother said, "That's some stone that you drew! It would be much better if you went to live with the Jew!" And Aunt Francisca said, "Shut up! The only innocent one in this whole mess is the boy!" And Grandfather said "The only important thing is that the Jew goes on sending you money every month."

# Chronicles: 1924

Don Augusto B. Leguía is reelected President of the Republic. There are conspiracies again; the number of men deported or in prison is multiplied.

An evening of theater organized by the Cultural Circle of Jewish Youth takes place in the hall of the Hebrew Union. Messrs. Shapiro, Metz, and Kaplan play in the one-act comedy "Oilam Habo," by Sholem Aleichem. Each is most satisfactory in his role, but Mr. Metz is outstanding as the mother, giving evidence of an obvious artistic vocation. The play is followed by a dance that goes on into the early hours of the morning.

On the afternoon of July 25, don Efraín Wilson Rebolledo visits Jacobo Lerner's store. As usual, he is astounded by the marvelous variety of cloth on the shelves. He feels as if he were in an Arab bazaar. Closing his eyes he thinks he perceives the sensual and exotic smell of spices, olives, and oil; he hears voices bargaining in a strange language. When the last customer leaves, don Efraín approaches the counter, smiling, and shakes hands firmly and energetically with Jacobo. After they exchange the usual polite questions and answers, he asks Jacobo to dinner at his house that evening. In spite of the warnings of León Mitrani, Jacobo Lerner leaves the hotel at eight-thirty, dressed in suit and tie. At that moment, almost unable to restrain her excitement, Bertila Wilson puts on a new dress.

Traffic in the Jewish Library for the month of July. Readers: 51. Books read in Yiddish: 16; in Hebrew: 4; in Spanish: 6. Total: 26.

The circumcision of Yosef Lerner by Rabbi Schneider takes place in the home of Mr. and Mrs. Lerner, 1274 Alfonso Ugarte Avenue. A large number of friends are present at the ceremony, and all are favorably impressed by the new rabbi.

SAN MARTIN HALL *

October 13, 1924—at 9 P.M.

In celebration of the traditional holiday of
SIMCHATH-TORAH

DIE FARGHESENE MAME
("The Forgotten Mother")
the well-received work by J. SEGAL
in 3 acts with music.

DIRECTION: Rubén Avidor

STARRING:
Marcos Kaplan, Clara Shapiro,
Julio Feldman and Miriam Abramowitz

POPULAR PRICES

Cultural Circle of Jewish Youth

# ON JEWS IN PERU

(Special for *Jewish Soul*)

There is no problem of antisemitism in Peru. Instead of manifesting itself as hatred against the Jew, that jingoist spirit of racial or cultural pride frequently occasions prejudice against the Asiatics or even against our very own Indians. This is a sad example of how man, hiding behind diverse excuses, strives constantly to forget the precept of "love one another."

DR. MANUEL PAZ SOLDAN

# MEMBERS OF OUR COMMUNITY

## SAMUEL EDELMAN

"I have love for our community in the blood," don Samuel Edelman once told us in conversation, and it is obviously so: don Samuel Edelman is a true "chalutz" (pioneer) among us, who from the earliest beginnings took it upon himself to insure that the Jewish community and institutions of Lima succeeded and prospered.

We can say with no fear of being mistaken that it is in great part thanks to the indefatigable labors of don Samuel that we have today the Hebrew Union in Lima. May God grant that don Samuel return here and settle again amongst us

The great Unamuno, speaking of Baruch Spinoza, said that "just as one feels physical pain in a limb, a hand or a tooth, and suffers from it, so Spinoza felt, and suffered, his God." Of Edelman we can say that he feels, and suffers, the Hebrew Union.

# III

## *Samuel Edelman: Chiclayo, November, 1935*

THE TALMUD says that everything has its time and its place so . . . no one could save Jacobo. A year without news. Why go see him? It's not worth it. He has his life, I mine. Thank God I received his letter in Chiclayo, if not I'd never have found out about his last will. Crazy man sent it to León's store after what happened. He must have lost his reason, to ask me to bring the boy to Lima now.

Don't go, Samuel, Felisa told me. I even told him myself, silently, inside myself, not to ask that, not to be crazy, to let things go their own way. It is too late, Jacobo, too late. Better spend your time preparing for death like a good Jew.

Felisa is dying of fear, and tomorrow she is not going to let me go. Because look, Samuel, she says, look at what they did to León in that village. The truth is they wished him evil, though I tell her he died of illness and I tell her if I go nothing is going to happen to me. It's my duty, I tell Felisa, it's my duty as a Jew. But she doesn't understand. I try to explain to her, but she doesn't understand.

Jacobo spent the best years of his life in the footsteps of his brother. He wanted everyone to love him, Sara too, but she wasn't about to look at him. Who was he? A nobody. That's why he wanted everyone to love him, gave money right and left. It's not bad to help Moisés, or Marquitos' widow, but to lend money to people who you know are not going to give it back is madness. Charity is one thing, and wasting money is another, says the Talmud.

It's not too late for him to put his life in order. No one should say at the moment of death that he is too busy with the obligations of his house, that tomorrow he will begin to take care of his soul. The spirit comes before the body, I would tell him that if I could see him, but first I have to go to Chepén, even if Felisa says for the love of God, Samuel, don't go. They don't remember me, woman, I tell her, I haven't been in that hell since León died.

What am I doing bringing his boy here? It's for friendship that I do it, I say to Felisa, he's suffered enough, otherwise I wouldn't go to Chepén for all the money in the world.

They killed León, Felisa says. Don't you realize, Samuel, she says, they killed León. Let's go to Lima, she says, so that we can live with your people.

What people, woman? I never went after the things that seduced Jacobo. Marry a Jewish woman? Fine. And if there aren't any? How long must one wait? How long must one live alone? I would have married Sara with my eyes closed. But marry Miriam? You have to be crazy. I wouldn't be at all surprised if Daniel killed himself because of her. Shame! It was a shame for the whole community! Thank God that Jacobo canceled the wedding. Miriam was only after his money. She was after my money too. She would have jumped at the chance if I had said, Miriam, do you want to be my wife? But you would have to be crazy. Better to marry a Christian than a bad Jewish woman. I told Jacobo, better to marry a Christian. But he never listened. He wouldn't even listen now, now that he's dying, poor man.

It's good to go to the synagogue when one believes in those things, but how many times men go to speak of business and women to show off their jewelry. I let Felisa go to church and pray to her saints all she wants, except not in front of the children. I want them to be Jewish. Otherwise, it's the same living here or living in Lima. There is no Jewish atmosphere in Lima. I told Felisa that to go to the Hebrew Union every once in a while to dance foxtrots, tangos, or rumbas has nothing to do with being Jewish. People go there like they go to a dance hall. But Felisa always asks, don't you miss your people, Samuel?

Jacobo, it was a mistake for you to leave Chepén, I told him a thousand times. I always brought him news of his boy, but it's not the same thing as having him by his side, taking care of him, and seeing him grow up strong and healthy, as it should be.

Why am I going? I don't know. Jacobo, it is better to forget Efraín. The boy is strange, Jacobo. He has strange things in his head. The boy is not well.

I never told him that I have a family, that I have Felisa and my children in Chiclayo. He has no one. León is dead, and Jacobo is dying alone.

It's been four years since I went to Chepén to see his boy. I'm sorry now I didn't bring Jacobo with me. Afterward, I didn't see Jacobo for a whole year. He looked like a ghost of himself, shrunken like the wrinkled, damp mushrooms that grew next to the river of my village. I went to give him the news that León had died, and all night I had to sit by his side. He himself smelled of death. He didn't want to leave the house, always wandering from room to room, like a ghost. Late in the afternoon he would go up to the roof and sit there with his head bent, lost in his thoughts. At night he locked himself in his room until the following morning. I couldn't talk to him about anything; he was lost, he had caught León's madness, always obsessed with Germans and pogroms. And if the Germans came to the house? he asked me one day. León had asked me the same question. And what could I answer?

Marquitos told me before he died that Moisés had stolen money from Jacobo, and now Jacobo had nothing left at all. I had warned him that nothing good could come from Moisés. Don't go back to Chepén, I had warned him, travel from village to village, the way I do.

So Jacobo became just like León. I loved him, León. I loved him as my brother, but it was a nightmare finally to stay in his house, the echo of his voice in empty rooms bringing back the past, and again the past. The Germans will come here too, he used to say. Some day, they will arrive here.

Everything was upside down in that house. The blind woman in her room, upstairs, praying with her rosary in her hands, and shaking, shaking all the time as if she were epileptic. León locked up in his room, shouting, speaking to invisible people about things I could never understand.

Now León's bones are somewhere, who knows where, in the open, without decent burial. Afterward I told Felisa that when I die please not to send the box to Lima, that I want to be buried here, in Chiclayo, and Felisa said it was a sad destiny not to be buried.

I told the priest not to send the box to Lima, to bury him there, in town, that I was going to give a good donation to the church. But all he could say was we should take him to some other graveyard. I couldn't send him to Guadalupe, because the priest there didn't like me very much either. He thought I was a communist. Father Chirinos asked me the same thing, if I was a communist. There was nothing else I could do. I had to send the box to Lima. I didn't want to have trouble with anyone.

Thank God I don't have to come back again to this village, I told myself. I'm going right back to Chiclayo now, good-bye to this town forever. That's why I went to old Wilson's house, because I knew that it was my last trip to Chepén.

I also knew that Jacobo would ask about Efraín. But after I had seen the boy I couldn't bring myself to tell him the truth. Nine years old and he looked like a shadow, skin and bones. It wasn't good to talk to him, I said to myself. If he didn't know about his father, it was better not to talk to him. Solomon said there is a time to speak and a time to be silent. What would I have said? It wasn't the time to tell the boy what had happened to his father.

The house was as cold as a cave, and the priest was there that day. I didn't see the boy's mother anywhere, but old man Wilson said I should take the boy to Lima with me, at once, he would be better off with his father. Perhaps he was right. But the priest interrupted him, said those were the words of the devil, it was a sin to send the boy to live with a Jew.

Jacobo could have gone to see him those times that he traveled to the north, but they would have killed him if he had gone into town. He only sold in Guadalupe and San Pedro and never showed his face in Chepén. He would have to be crazy to appear at the Wilson's house after what had happened and doña Jesús hating him the way she did.

It was a crazy house too. I thought they were going to kill me when I was there.

And now, after all this time, Jacobo asks me to bring him his son. I promised Felisa that I would never return to Chepén after León died.

When I went to tell him that León had died Jacobo didn't want his son to stay in Chepén any more, and he told me to go and offer them money in exchange for the boy. The boy is better there, now, I thought to myself, besides, they'll kick me out. You don't buy a boy with money or with merchandise. Efraín, poor boy, was so sad he looked as if he didn't belong in this world. He seemed almost dead. Perhaps he is dead, already. It is stupid to go now, after so much time has gone by. Let him stay there, I told him.

No, said Jacobo. Sara will be his mother. Where could he have got that idea? What is Sara going to do with Efraín? The only thing she ever felt for Jacobo was compassion, and perhaps gratitude because he saved Moisés from jail and ruin, but she never felt love for him, the way he believes.

It is time Jacobo marries and raises a family, Sara said to me one day. It is not a good thing for a man to live alone, and Miriam would make a good wife. Thank God Jacobo opened his eyes. Even then, he could have made a better life for himself, a decent life, fit for a Jew, not like he has now, in a brothel. It is not fit for a Jew, I would tell him if I could go to see him. It is time to repent one's sins, I would tell him.

So what? What other Jews are doing is even worse. Last year, Lubin set fire to his store, and Fishman is a smuggler. His picture is in all the papers, shaming the whole community. Community? There's no interest in the community. There is no charity. There is no Jewish culture. The library is empty. Don't they realize that good books are like a tonic prescribed by a doctor?

That's why it's good I came to Chiclayo to raise my family, even if I don't live among Jews. Let Moisés be the president and let him become rich and respected by everyone; for me, it's better to live in peace with my family. The first thing a shipwreck victim does as soon as he is on land is find company, someone with whom to face the dangers. That's why I married Felisa, and I have my children. Let Moisés be president. Who wants to finish like Daniel, full of debts and shooting himself in the head? Or like Jacobo, without anyone to pity his luck, not even his brother? But the least I could do is go to Chepén tomorrow and try to do what he asked me. . . .

# MEDICAL COLUMN

This new section, which will be in the very capable hands of Dr. Bernardo Rabinowitz, the well-known Jewish specialist, is included with the intent of popularizing medical knowledge of unquestioned utility for the community.

—The Editors

## DIGESTIVE PROBLEMS

There are countless people who, though still young, have been aged prematurely by digestive problems, to the point that they have lost interest in life because of heartburn, vomiting, abdominal pains after meals, frequent indigestion, headaches, skin eruptions, inexplicable diarrhea, insatiable appetite, hemorrhoids, dizziness, coated tongue, bad breath, etc.

It is easy to avoid these disturbances by observing certain principles of hygiene. The first is to eat at regular hours, and to chew slowly. At meal times, worry should be avoided at all costs.

As far as the kind of foods that should be consumed one should not overindulge in spicy or fatty foods, particularly stews, sauces, liverwurst, brains, tripe, sausages, blood sausages, sweetbreads, sea food, game, etc.

It is not a good idea to eat meat, white or dark to excess. Therefore, only one meat dish should be served at each meal, accompanied by vegetables. The second dish could be spaghetti, mashed potatoes, or spinach with melted butter.

(To be continued)

# ON JEWS IN PERU

(Exclusive for *Jewish Soul*)

Under the title "How the Holy Office of Lima Turned a Jew into a Saint," don José A. Lavalle has published some facts about the Venerable Antonio de San Pedro, whose secular name was Antonio Rodríguez Correa. He was a peddler of colonial times, a seller of yarn and buttons, who, condemned, was secluded in the convent of San José, to work in the kitchen. Sent to the Old World, he became a lay brother, and helped along both by his mystical bent and by the delicate religious sensuality of the city (that also fanned the mystical flame of Fray Martín of Porres), he spread good deeds and counsel to all those who came in contact with him, as if a living example of the proverb of Rabbi don Santos:

> The hawk is not worth the less
> because in a dirty nest it live;
> good counsel God does bless
> even though a Jew might give . . .

A book entitled *Prodigious God in the Obstinate Jew,* published in Lima in 1692, says the following:

"Antonio de San Pedro practiced the Mosaic Law, even though he had been baptized, keeping the Sabbath, praying the Psalms of David without the gloria patri, and keeping a Bible in the vulgate. He committed several heresies. During his trip to Huancavelica he recited a prayer that, according to him, had the power of warding off all dangers, and he advised his companions to imitate him. In Lima, he met with others of his sect to celebrate

28

the great day of the Lord in the manner of the Hebrews, that is to say, reciting psalms, eating stewed fish with oil, and bread without leavening."

FRAY FERNANDO,
Lay Brother of the Convent
of La Merced

# IV

CONFINED TO his sickbed by strict orders of Doctor Rabinowitz, Jacobo Lerner spent several days patiently putting his papers in order. He worked without rest until very late at night, verifying extremely old bills and going over, in his head, the inventory of the house. Meanwhile, a powdery ashen dust filtered through doors and windows, accumulating in every room.

When he saw that he was not leaving any debts behind, Jacobo felt something between annoyance and rancor, but consoled himself with the idea that, as long as he was alive, no one, not even his brother Moisés, would come into his house to disturb the strict and rigorous order he had imposed in the last six years.

Everything was in its place: on the roof, countless pots held ivy, gardenias, geraniums, and carnations, and the canaries and nightingales still sang their songs in their gigantic cage; in the living room, the armchairs covered in a flowered material, the same ones that he had bought at the suggestion of his sister-in-law after his second return to Lima, were undisturbed with their plump, dusty cushions; in the dining room, no one sat at any of the eight chairs upholstered in red velvet around the heavy, dark table; in his study, where he had sat at night at his accounts in front of the old walnut desk, the books were still on their shelves, the backs of most still unbroken; in the bedroom, the Louis XVI bed on which he lay, whose purchase doña Juana had recommended, and everything else that was familiar, the night-table with the radio bought in installments in 1929, the dressing table with the ornamented silver candelabra and the blue earthenware elephant, and, against the far wall, covering it almost completely, the heavy wardrobe.

As soon as he had finished the inventory, Jacobo Lerner painfully raised himself on his elbows, half turned around, and made sure that the portrait of his parents still hung above the bed. Then he let himself drop back onto the bed, and he closed his eyes. He tried to shoo from his mind a swarm of memories that bothered his spirit, but he could not. For several weeks he had felt himself racing vertiginously through time, dragged from scene to scene like a puppet. His life seemed like a trip that began in Chepén and ended in Staraya Ushitza, in front of the abandoned body of his father, and as if Lima were a weightless region somewhere between these two spaces.

When he remembered that in 1926 he had been swindled by his brother Moisés, that for two years he had traveled through inhospitable villages and that, in 1934, he had been possessed by the spirit of León Mitrani, Jacobo thought he had lived all this time defenseless against an all-powerful enemy whose amusement it was to pursue him without mercy. And now he saw himself cornered by death. He knew he was going to die without getting to know his son, that he could not harbor the hope that his life would be continued by an heir. On several occasions he had tried to imagine the face of his son, but the sometimes threatening, sometimes shy visage of Bertila always interposed itself. The vague, melancholy memory of a tenuous happiness in the Russian village of his birth, a happiness that he had never regained, forced him to think of God as a pitiless and arbitrary tyrant.

When at last he managed to fall asleep, Jacobo dreamed that he was visited by Moisés, León, and Samuel. Having arranged to come and scold him, the three took up positions around the bed and again and again asked him why he had abandoned his son into the hands of Christians. They told him all his suffering was punishment for wrongs committed and the only thing he could do now, at the hour of his death, was to turn toward God with a repentant soul. But Jacobo defended his own innocence and when the attacks by his visitors became sharper he begged them, with his voice tearful and spent, to leave him alone to die in peace. He told them that divine justice was a fantasy, because both the wicked and the just perished in the hands of God.

When he woke up from his dream Jacobo was troubled by restless thoughts that flew through his mind like birds of ill omen. On a similar night full of the smell of burnt cooking oil and sounds of rhythmic music, Samuel Edelman had come to his house to give him the news of León Mitrani's death. In the nine years since he had left Chepén, there had been only silence between him and his friend, Mitrani.

After he learned the news of Mitrani's death, Jacobo lit seven candles on seven consecutive days and went to the synagogue of Breña to say *kaddish* for his dead friend. Without any indications other than those provided by his imagination, Jacobo Lerner thought that his life, as well as Mitrani's, could have been very different if fortune had only smiled on them. He also thought it was most probable Mitrani had been buried under a cross.

His memory returned to the year 1917. It was Saturday night, and he was going with León Mitrani to Rabbi Finkelstein's. He carried his prayerbook under his arm, because they were both preparing for their *bar-mitzvah* that would take place the following year. Among the children of their age there were none who knew the Bible better than they, and the two friends dreamed that some day they would become serious scholars of the Talmud, perhaps respected and wise rabbis of communities larger and more important than Staraya Ushitza, with Rabbi Finkelstein's daughters as wives.

Then came the years of the first war, in which the rabbi's school was closed, and an epidemic of hunger was visited upon the village.

In 1917, after his sister Judith and her son had disappeared, after her husband had gone crazy and Jacobo's parents had died, the Germans came into Staraya Ushitza. That was the year in which Mitrani's father also died. León had been insulted by Rabbi Finkelstein in the middle of the street and in the hearing of many people, as a consequence of which he had left the study of the Talmud and lived as a recluse, without leaving his house.

That same year, Mitrani became friendly with Yehuda Moretz, a carpenter who had arrived in the village with a group of refugees from Lithuania. Moretz told about the advance of the Bolshevik troops and convinced Mitrani that they should go to meet them. A few months later Mitrani entered the socialist ranks in which he actively participated until 1920, the year in which he returned to his mother's house disillusioned, and had made the irrevocable decision to leave Russia.

Jacobo Lerner had stayed behind in the village, and he had taken care of Mitrani's mother. In 1917 and in 1919 he witnessed pogroms. Finally, in 1920, he decided to leave Russia with his friend.

Going up the Dnieper River, Jacobo and León arrived at Kiev in a fishing boat. From there they went by train to Koresten. Since they had no passports, they got in touch with the son of the rabbi there who agreed, for a price of ten rubles, to take them illegally to the city of Krakov, on the Polish side. All night they walked through a thick wood, always fearful that they might be discovered by the soldiers who patrolled the border. Once they were safely in Krakov, they did not stay long, but went directly to Warsaw where they obtained false passports to get into Germany.

Jacobo Lerner and León Mitrani separated in Hamburg, where the latter shipped off to Brazil as a sailor on the S.S. *Bremen*. Worried about relatives he had left behind in Russia, Lerner decided to wait a while in Germany.

A year later, without knowing that Mitrani had ended up in Peru, Jacobo Lerner arrived at the port of Callao. What happened afterward was coincidence. In the rooming house at Jesús María, where he was staying, he met Samuel Edelman, a tall, strongly built Jew from Vinnitsa, a village about fifteen leagues away from Staraya Ushitza. Edelman told him that in a small town in the north, about five hundred kilometers from Lima, lived a countryman of his whose name was Mitrani.

# VICTIMS OF THE INQUISITION

(Exclusive for *Jewish Soul*)

## MANUEL LOPEZ

He was accused of keeping the Sabbath, of sweeping the house and putting on a clean shirt before sundown on Friday, and of telling a friend stories about the people of Israel.

The Tribunal condemned him to be paraded in the streets bound and gagged, and his goods were confiscated.

Subjected to torture to make him confess his beliefs, he admitted under pain that he was a Jew.

He remained loyal to his faith, and was then sentenced to be burned alive.

Having died in jail before the sentence was executed, his remains were publicly burned by the Inquisition.

FRAY FERNANDO,
Lay Brother of the Convent
of La Merced

---

# NOTICE

MANY OF US HAVE BECOME OR ARE BECOMING PERUVIAN CITIZENS. WE EMBRACE OUR NEW NATIONALITY BECAUSE WE WANT TO MAKE TIGHTER THE BOND THAT TIES US TO OUR HOME AND NOT FOR ANY PROFIT IT MIGHT BRING US.

JEW, BECOME A PERUVIAN CITIZEN!

# READERS' FORUM

Chiclayo, January, 1925

To the Editors

Dear Sirs:
It is well known that those countries where the Jewish colony is large profit not only from its participation in commerce, but in the arts and sciences as well. Although our colony here is young it is already possible to note its great influence. Many commercial houses in Lima have Jewish names, as do several industries in areas such as textiles, furs, and others that were not exploited before we came.

Many Jews, in witness of gratitude and affection to this great country that has hospitably opened its doors to us have become naturalized citizens, and will pass our nationality down to our children. Many others who have not yet done this have nonetheless built their homes in this land that they love as a second country, and are willing to adapt themselves to its customs and way of life.

I am, gentlemen, your most obedient servant,

SAMUEL EDELMAN

# NOTICE

THE STEERING COMMITTEE OF THE HEBREW
UNION NOTIFIES THE COMMUNITY that the matzos
ordered from the famous house of Manischewitz (New York)
have been received. They will be sold at the following stores:

DANIEL ABRAMOWITZ, Plateros de
San Pedro 188
MOISES ZIGEL, Espíritu Santo 543
AARON PECK, General La Fuente 194

Please address all orders from the provinces to don Moisés
Lerner, Bodegones 393, Lima, including a postal money order
for the amount plus transport.

# AUTOS-DA-FE

(Exclusive for *Jewish Soul*)

When the Holy Office started its terrifying work in Lima, autos-da-fé, the public burning of renegades or heretics, took place in all the main squares. Soon, however, the barbarous spectacle was moved away from the central area of the city toward the new settlements that encompassed it with high and solid walls of adobe.

The burnings could last from the earliest hours of the morning to the late afternoon, depending on how many had been sentenced to the torment of the flames.

The accompanying ceremonies were solemn in the extreme and gave guests the opportunity of wearing orders, decorations, and insignia. The High Marshal, the Secretaries, the Ministers of the Tribunal and their families arrived on horseback preceded by trumpets, clarions, and drums, and by the crier who announced the crimes and punishments.

Then came the standard, itself followed by many dignitaries. The Vicar General of Santo Domingo wore the green cross, behind him hooded monks carried flaming torches. The choir of the Main Church sang "Virilia Regis" and "Deus Laudem Tuam," and then came the governors, their rank indicated by their black staffs.

The penitents came into the square from the other side, carrying the cross of the parish, and aided by a group of priests singing "Miserere Mei."

Finally the Viceroy arrived, with his group of soldiers and lancers and his court of gentlemen.

The bells rang lugubriously while they placed the condemned on the stake, tied them down, and began the burning.

FRAY FERNANDO,
Lay Brother of the Convent
of La Merced

37

# MEDICAL COLUMN

## MORE ON DIGESTIVE PROBLEMS

Regular, daily movement of the bowels must become a habit early in life with the help of physical exercise and an appropriate diet. Laxatives and other purgative agents, taken alone, often do nothing more than aggravate whatever problems may exist.

Overexcitement of any kind is inimical to the digestive processes, and must be avoided whenever possible.

Crash diets, so popular these days, are extremely dangerous since they can lower our resistance to such diseases as tuberculosis, or at best are the cause of stomach troubles.

Tight girdles change the shape of our internal organs and inhibit normal breathing. It is preferable that girdles be comfortable to wear and that they not be too high above the abdomen.

Remember, it is not enough to live. It is necessary to know how to live.

DR. BERNARDO RABINOWITZ

# V

WHENEVER HE went into León Mitrani's house, Jacobo Lerner felt that he had tumbled, arms flailing, into a world where everything was at once strange and familiar. Faded engravings of the Saint of Motupe, shiny chromos of the Sacred Heart of Jesus, and wooden crucifixes of all sizes were arranged side by side with bronze candelabra, a red philactery bag on which the star of David was embroidered in gold, and several *sidurim* with tooled leather covers that Mitrani had taken from his father's house.

The first time Jacobo Lerner saw these relics he thought about his own father who had died in Staraya Ushitza, in snow and loneliness, and wondered whether Abraham, his brother, still had the old man's things.

In that large old house of passageways, of closed rooms, of spacious interior gardens that appeared to float in rarefied air, where it seemed necessary to move in silence and with head bent as if marching in a procession, Jacobo Lerner always felt oppressed by windows that were always closed, by narrow hallways that led nowhere; he felt locked in a world of armchairs worn by use and chests redolent of moths and mothballs.

Mitrani's wife, who had gradually gone blind in spite of the efforts of doctors and medical science, lived on the top floor of the house. There she had a room apart from her husband's, where she spent most of her time sewing throws and pillow covers, which he then sold at modest prices in his store.

Once, lost in the labyrinths of that old house, Jacobo went into her room by mistake, and stood by the door while, unaware of his presence, she recited a litany in a barely audible voice: "Lord, forgive me for not having followed your precepts; for having given my body to a heretic who blasphemes your name, forgive me. Lord, please try to understand, who will take pity on me, now, old and blind as I am? Who will take me into his house? Lord, I repent, I will always repent falling into temptation, Lord, repent having disobeyed my father, repent having not set foot in a church since I came to live in this house. Forgive me, oh God, I have even thought of killing him. I have stayed awake nights planning how to kill him. Forgive, oh Lord, and hear the prayer of this, your wayward sheep; take her unto your kingdom."

When Jacobo told Mitrani about the incident, he shrugged his shoulders and said he knew his wife was crazy. Later he warned Jacobo, in a threatening tone, not to meddle in what did not concern him. Jacobo was very disturbed, not so much because he had been told off in such an insulting manner, but because of the lackadaisical way in which his friend had received the news. That particular conversation confirmed the suspicions that had been taking shape in his mind since his arrival in Chepén. If it was true that the wife was not sound and sane, it was also true that León was not far behind. Lately, he had taken to getting up at the first glint of dawn to put on the philacteries that had been his father's and his grandfather's before him.

Absurd, thought Jacobo, how absurd that León, who had been publicly vilified by the rabbi of his village because he had not been present to say *kaddish* for his father after having renounced the religion of his ancestors, should now, an old man, become a punctilious observer of religious ritual. He had even begun to study the Torah again, and sometimes, no matter where he was, he spoke of Isaiah and his prophet's fury against the King of Judea for having bled his people, sacked the Temple of Solomon, abolished Hebrew as the kingdom's official language, and instituted the adoration of Assyrian gods, all for the sake of appeasing Tiglat, the invader. As was to be expected, Mitrani's behavior not only frightened the people of the village but also required the intervention of Father Chirinos. The priest's admonitions, however, had little effect on the spirit of Mitrani, since they issued, he claimed, from an imposter. Did he not, after all, represent a god whose existence, both celestial and eternal, had been doubted as early as the thirteenth century by Abraham Ibn Ezra, the Judeo-Hispanic poet?

It was about this time that people stopped going to Mitrani's store, and gradually his friends abandoned him as well. Out of necessity, Mitrani's old customers ended up patronizing Jacobo Lerner's store, where, if it was true that they might not find what they needed, at least they were certain of not being accosted and insulted in the language of a cheap brothel.

After a while, Jacobo was the only one who dared speak to Mitrani. When they met each other in public, in the lobby of the hotel where Jacobo lived or on a bench in the little park across the street from the hotel, Jacobo tried as hard as he could to keep the conversation in Yiddish and in that way disappoint the expectations of all those who stopped to listen. But, invariably, Mitrani would end up speaking the impeccable Spanish that he had learned by assiduously reading the Spanish version of the New Testament. This command of the language, which now carried the meaning of his words to all those who were eagerly listening, had been the sole result of his wife's efforts to teach him the true doctrine.

No wonder, then, that Jacobo decided to limit his sporadic visits to either his own small hotel room or Mitrani's house. Even when it became almost impossible to deal with his friend, Jacobo still derived a certain satisfaction from going to see him in that big old house where the sun, instead of giving light, seemed to make all objects dark.

By then, most conversations were nothing more than incoherent perorations about Mitrani's frustrated career in the Bolshevik ranks in 1920, but Jacobo still liked to hear him speak of that period when they lived together in that distant Ukrainian village. There were many things that tied them one to the

41

other. They had been born in the same year. Together they had gone to school at Rabbi Finkelstein's, and together they had their *bar-mitzvah* in the synagogue. They had left Russia together, crossing the police border on foot, and now, after a separation of three years, they were together again in the godforsaken town of Chepén.

But friendship was not the only reason Jacobo went to Mitrani's house. In a room that looked over an uncared-for garden that had become the domain of weeds, Mitrani kept a few books in Yiddish and Russian. While Mitrani slept in the afternoon, a habit that he had learned to keep religiously, Jacobo read novels by Isaac Peretz, Sholem Asch, and Sholem Aleichem. Among those volumes of yellowed, cracking sheets, he found a coverless edition of *The Eternal Jew*, a play by David Pinsky that had been performed in Moscow by the "habimah" company around 1916. But his favorites were the novels of Sholem Aleichem, especially *The Death of Yankel Brodsky* that told what happened to a Jewish family in Czarist Russia.

What he read those afternoons, reminiscing with León Mitrani, and an old portrait of his parents that he kept packed at the bottom of his suitcase were the only contacts Jacobo Lerner had with a past that was quickly breaking into small fragments as days went by in Chepén.

# VI

THE PHOTOGRAPH showed a tall, thin man wearing a dark coat and a wide-brimmed hat. He was leaning on a cane, and a thick white beard fell, raddled, halfway down his chest. Next to him, sitting on the edge of an armchair covered in some flowered material, was a small woman with her hands crossed on her lap. Her face was drawn and her eyes were sad. Her hair was covered by a kerchief. The photograph had been taken in Minsk the day the whole family had gone to witness Aunt Natasha's marriage to Leopoldo Myshkin, a man of heavy limbs and disproportionately large head which was crowned by a shiny bald pate. The wedding took place in 1905, when Jacobo was only ten years old and incapable of imagining that ten years later he would begin to watch the progressive disintegration of his family.

First there was the mysterious disappearance of his sister Judith. Judith left the village with her six-year-old son in the middle of the war to look for her husband Mishka, who, according to the letter received from the military authorities, was convalescing in a hospital in a not too distant city. There was never any further news of either of them. Judith's husband, who had lost his right arm, crisscrossed the Ukraine on foot, trying to locate his wife and son. After several long months of futile search, he showed up one day at the Lerner house, completely defeated. His clothing was filthy and ragged, his face was sallow, his beard dirty, and his back bent.

Hunger and desperation had driven him mad, and he spent the rest of his days in the asylum at Poltrava.

Jacobo's father died the following year. He had gone to a nearby village to sell a few bags of oats and was found frozen on the road where his wagon had lost a wheel. Two months later, his wife followed, dying in her sleep at the age of fifty-five.

Without any family ties to keep them there, the three Lerner brothers decided to go their own ways. Abraham, the eldest, ended up in New York where, in time, he opened a furrier's shop in Brooklyn, married, and had three children. Jacobo stayed in the village, living in the house of León Mitrani. Moisés, the youngest of the three, went to live in Minsk, where he was warmly received by Aunt Natasha.

Jacobo and Moisés saw each other again in 1922, in Lima. Until 1923 they worked as peddlers in the streets of the city, selling razor blades, cheap bracelets, necklaces made from glass beads, and other trinkets. During this time they lived in a rooming house in the quarter of Jesús María, run by Madame Chernigov, a Russian countess who had seen better days. It was toward the end of this period that Jacobo Lerner received the letter from León Mitrani. Since he had been able to save a modest amount of capital, and since Moisés was planning to marry a Jewish woman from Vienna, Jacobo decided to follow his friend's advice and move to Chepén.

After living in Chepén for a year, Jacobo Lerner met Bertila, a seventeen-year-old girl with a gypsy cast to her face. She was the second daughter of don Efraín Wilson Rebolledo, a tall, red-faced man of English and Spanish blood, and of doña Jesús Alvarado, a dark-skinned lady with a tendency to gain weight, whose ancestors had been Andalucian and Indian. Bertila, who had never set foot outside of Chepén, fell in love with Jacobo Lerner the first time she saw him. She would look at him from across the street while he worked in his store, half-hiding among the bags of peanuts piled in front of Chang's grocery.

Since Jacobo had become the topic of dinner conversation in most of the houses of the village, Bertila had already heard of him, particularly from Efraín Wilson, who used to refer to him as "the Jew" not without a certain admiration, because, as he said, he was a businessman himself and respected "men of enterprise." Besides, the old man considered himself an Anglo-Saxon, choosing to forget his Hispanic side, and imagined that between him and Jacobo Lerner there was a link: they were both foreigners and both had the firm intention of increasing their wealth as quickly as possible by abstaining from unnecessary luxuries.

Don Efraín Wilson Rebolledo had moved to Chepén after the death of his father from whom he inherited a considerable sum of money and a capacity for hard work. Married and already the father of a daughter, the first thing he did when he arrived in the village was to buy a house on the main street. With time, don Efraín acquired more children and more houses. He owned twenty-five by the time Jacobo began courting Bertila, and their combined rents were more than thirty-five hundred *soles.* If one added to this the income from his trips to nearby villages, where he sold basins, pots, paraffin stoves, kerosene lamps, china, and almost everything else that might be of use in the house, one might finally come to consider him a wealthy man.

The more León Mitrani neglected his business, the more Jacobo Lerner prospered. His financial success intensified the original curiosity don Efraín had felt toward him, and one night don Efraín went to his store to ask him to dinner.

That same night, Jacobo was formally introduced to Bertila. Despite the natural shyness of the girl, they got along very well from the moment they met. As soon as she felt slightly more at ease, Bertila began to ask him question after question about his travels through the world and the people he had met. Since he did not think his life had been in any way exceptional, Jacobo Lerner seasoned his adventures with wholly invented incidents. After a while, he found he could make Bertila believe him without difficulty, and so he convinced her, among other things, that he had been a soldier in the world war, that he had gone on pilgrimage to the Holy Sepulcher, and that he had been present at the opening of the Panama Canal. Bertila had never received any kind of formal schooling as the village school had opened when she was in her early

45

teens, and Jacobo had to explain to her what each of these names meant. Only religious topics required no explanation, because Bertila, who could read a little, loved to exercise this skill with the Bible. So, lying on the cot that he had set up in the back room of the store, Jacobo also told her a hundred times of the love of David and Bathsheba and of Samson and Delilah. Bertila listened, charmed by that voice that seemed to transport her to where all these marvelous events had taken place.

Jacobo, who had just turned twenty-nine, and whose sexuality had, until that moment, found satisfaction only in a few encounters with streetwalkers in Berlin, did not believe that a man could be so content.

# READERS' FORUM

Lima, April, 1925

To the Editor

Dear Sir:
I refer to the letter that appeared in the last issue of *Jewish Soul* on the fate of the library of the Hebrew Union. Knowing how important said library is to the community and having no desire to see it disappear, I would like to inform you that in many Jewish houses there are books that belong to the library. I think that it would be a good idea to name a commission (I have no objections at all to being a member) to visit all the Jewish houses of Lima in order to pick up all the books that belong to the library.
I remain, sir, yours sincerely,

MOISES LERNER

---

# CULTURAL EVENTS

## WHERE IS MY SON?

*Where is my Son?*, a musical drama in four acts, was presented last week at Bolognesi Hall. Though it is not a first-rate piece, it offers numerous opportunities for excellent

47

acting, and in spite of deficiencies in the sets, lighting, costumes, and other areas necessary for good theater, it was well received by the audience.

From the moment the curtain went up, one was conscious of the work of the director. There were highlights, however, in which it was more evident, such as the scene in the third act where Mother Peisajovich and Albert sing "Wi is main kind?" while the rest of the cast goes through the door making questioning gestures. There was considerable applause at the conclusion of the number.

Miss Guinsburg, in spite of acting, as we all know, under the handicap of a severe attack of influenza, distinguished herself in her portrayal of a woman physically and morally ruined, having indulged in all the vices, including drink. The early scenes of the play, in which the character was inebriated, were particularly successful.

Mr. Goldstein acted very well at the beginning of the play, evoking a lot of laughter as he fleshed out his comic role. Brassler was adequate as the doctor, but when reading the letter from his wife, who had abandoned him years before, he was not convincing and did not take advantage of this high point in the drama. Neither with his voice nor with his gestures did he manage to convey the feelings that, surely, were necessary at this point. Later, in the third act, when he sang "Wi is main kind?" he kept a cigar in his mouth, and even bent down his head, perhaps to hide a smile or some other sign of contempt for the work.

The performance of the musicians, finally, was not all that could have been desired. Nonetheless, the spectators left their seats pleased to have seen a work in Yiddish on a topic of extreme importance for all of us, that of a father trying to rescue his son from a mother ruined by vice, and facing all kinds of adversities in the process.

—THE EDITORS

# VII

## *Efraín: Chepén, January, 1933*

DOCTOR MENESES came this afternoon to see about my dizzy spells. Doctor Meneses is an old man, but not as old as Grandfather. He has long, yellowed nails, thick, bushy eyebrows like brambles, and wears black-rimmed glasses with thick lenses that make his eyes seem larger and rounder. I'm afraid of him because I have never seen him smile, and because he has a deep, hoarse voice like an ogre. Each time he examines me he becomes very serious and thoughtful, knits his brows, walks back a few steps, shakes his head several times and then just stares at me as if it were time for them to take me to the graveyard. Ricardo is also afraid of him, but he never gets sick, so he doesn't ever have to go to his office, which is crowded with glass cases full of foul-smelling medicines. He even has a skeleton that hangs from the ceiling like a hanged man.

I get sick all the time. Bertila says that I am a weakling and that I look like a scarecrow. Everyone in the house calls me scarecrow now. It must be because my legs are so thin and long that they look like stilts.

Last year I had bronchitis, whooping cough, and an intestinal fever, so I was absent from school almost the whole winter, but I didn't fall behind in my studies because I read the textbook all by myself, without anyone helping me. When I went back to school Miss Angelita was open-mouthed with surprise at how well I read and she promoted me to the third grade. She said I would only waste time in the second, even if that is Ricardo's grade, and Ricardo is two years older than I am, and my uncle. Iris is thirteen and she is only in the fourth grade because she doesn't like to study and prefers to cut school with Chang's daughters. They go down to the river in the afternoon, and Ricardo says that he has seen them bathing in the nude and they aren't even ashamed. They sit in the sand, touching their things, and once they showed him the hairs that Iris has and he felt ticklish in his whole body and blushed· scarlet. Grandmother has told Iris to be careful, because there is a demon who lives in the river who steals young girls and takes them to live in a castle deep under the water. When they come out again their bellies are so swollen that they can't even walk.

But the only illness I have now is my dizzy spells. I don't remember when they started, but Grandfather says I was born with them. Iris says when I was born I almost died. She says I used to choke so that I shook my whole body, like a worm, and my face would turn as red as any tomato. Doctor Meneses says there is no reason to worry, the dizzy spells are normal, and they come because I am growing. Ricardo turns green with envy when he hears this, because he is not too tall. The one bad thing about it is that they are giving me vitamins again and a spoonful of cod-liver oil every morning. I really don't like to take it, because it makes me gag, and sometimes even throw up. Then Bertila gets furious and screams that it doesn't matter to her if I die, if that's what I want. Bertila has gone to Lima now, though. It's been a week she's been gone. She said that there is no justice in this world but she would come back with her purse full of money and that from now on our luck would turn. I don't know where she expected to get the money, but that's what she said, rubbing her hands together like Grandfather when he makes a good business deal. Bertila left wearing her best dress. It really fits her and makes her look younger. Everyone in the village stares at her when she has it on. She also wore high heels, painted her eyebrows, had on deep red lipstick, and put powder all over her face so that you couldn't see her wrinkles. Bertila always says life has knocked her around and that's why she looks like an old woman.

She doesn't like my dizzy spells, and she doesn't like my headaches, either. I don't get headaches as often, anymore. I used to get them everywhere, in church, in school, even in the street when I was playing ball with my friends and I least expected them. Now, when I get them I almost always get them at night, before I go to bed. They come suddenly, with no warning, as if a stroke of lightning had hit me on the head. Then I squirm in the bed with pain and bite my knuckles so that I don't cry out, but if I pull the covers over me, and curl up into a ball, with my hands between my legs, it doesn't last very long, and I can go to sleep without saying anything to Bertila. I don't like her to know because she scolds me, and then I dream the whole night of ghosts that come down from a tree and come and get me in the room. Sometimes they drag me out to the sty to roll around in the mud and eat garbage and grunt like the pigs.

When I get sick for several days, like now, Bertila calls Aunt Francisca to take care of me. Aunt Francisca sits for hours by the side of the bed, feeling my forehead to see if I have a fever, helping me eat my soup, cleaning my face with a wet cloth and telling me stories. She tells me about the time when they lived in Cajamarca and she almost married one of her father's countrymen, a tall, good-looking gentleman. Her life would have been different then, she says. She would have had her own house and her own children. She wouldn't have had to look after Grandfather's strongbox, and she wouldn't have had to wipe Uncle Pedro's ass. That's what Aunt Francisca says, and she also says, sighing, that she wishes I were her son. She's gone to the market now, to do the shopping, and she is going to bring me some oranges. Grandmother says that orange peel boiled in salt water is a good medicine against dizzy spells. I want to get better so I can go down to the river and see Chang's daughters with their bellies swollen. Grandmother says boiled orange peel is a family remedy, and then Grandfather smiles and says that Grandmother's mother was a bit of a witch, and that they stoned her out of Cajamarca because she was putting spells on half the town and people would die without warning and no one knew why. But Grandfather is a liar of the worst kind and I don't believe anything he says. About a month ago he said we were going to move to a bigger house with balconies that gave out onto the street, a big attic where we could play hide and seek, and an orchard with avocados and fruit trees and flowers, like the one Father Chirinos has behind the church. Finally, after all that, he rented it to the brother of don Fermín, the owner of the hardware store. Whenever I give don Fermín a handful of rusty nails that I get from the bottom of the irrigation ditch he gives me a coin, and I bury it, so that Bertila will not spend it.

Once, Grandfather promised that he would take us to Pacasmayo to visit Irma. I was very happy because I thought that at last I would see the ocean and I could roll in the sand at the beach. My uncle César says that the sand at the beach is as golden and fresh as wheat, and that when the sun shines on it, it glows like a medallion of the Virgin of Charity. My uncle César was away from the village for two years while he was in the army, and he has traveled a lot. I think he has even been to Lima. I'm never going to leave this village to see the ocean, because no one takes me anywhere, though now Grandfather has promised we will go to Pacasmayo next year. We can't go now because Irma is pregnant, and she prefers no one go to visit her because she is afraid of the evil eye. Only Bertila can go to see her because she helps her clean house and keeps her company. Grandmother says Irma's husband is always partying somewhere and leaves her all by herself. But Irma doesn't want to return home because of her pride, and because of what Grandmother said about one of her daughters dying and how she does not receive dead bodies in her house.

When Bertila comes back from Lima I am going to ask her to take me to Pacasmayo. I know that the engineer of Las Cruces always takes her in his truck to see the ocean. I'm frightened of looking at him in the face because he has a long scar on his cheek, but anyway I would like to go, and there is room in the truck for all of us, because I am sure that Iris and Ricardo would like to go too. I know what Bertila will say, though. She'll say I'm too young so she doesn't have to take me with her, or maybe she'll say I shouldn't be absent from school, or there is no room for me at Irma's house. I know Bertila likes to go away alone. Like this time, she has gone to Lima without saying a word to me, and if it weren't for Aunt Francisca I would never have found out. No one tells me anything in this house, only Ricardo sometimes invents stories to bother me. He said Bertila was not coming back, that she had found a husband in Lima. Later, when he thought the joke had gone far enough, he told me not to cry, that Bertila was going to bring me a white satin shirt and a blue suit for my first communion. That will be next month. I am going to be the best-dressed boy in the village. Let's see what the daughters of don Polo Miranda have to say then.

Aunt Francisca says that if every afternoon I went to church after school, the way Father Chirinos wants me to, all my dizzy spells would disappear because "great is the power of God." I promised her that from now on I am always going to carry the scapulary that Grandmother gave me, and each time I feel a headache coming on I will do exactly what Father Chirinos told me to do: I am going to say three Our Fathers and one Hail Mary. I am also going to read all about the saints in the images, because Father Chirinos says they were exemplary men and women. I know about Saint Michael, with his shining sword like the one Mr. Mitrani says will chop our heads off when he preaches on Sunday in front of the church. But Saint Michael is "the angel of the church, the captain of all of the troops of heaven." I also know about Saint Agueda, who has a palm leaf in one hand and a tray with two breasts in the other, because she was "a heroine of primitive Christianity and a slave of Christ, to whom she dedicated body and soul." That is what's written on the back of the image. Aunt Francisca also says I will have no more dizzy spells after my first communion because the body of Christ will enter my own and will frighten away all the evil spirits that are there. There must be many, she says, because they don't let me be, night or day. If I am awake I am dizzy, and if I am asleep they appear in my dreams so that I wake up thirsty, with cramps, and sweating.

I don't like to faint because I might die without anyone noticing it; or worse, they might think that I am dead when I am only asleep, and they might bury me alive.

"This must have something to do with the Jews, because no one in my family ever had such strange diseases," says Grandfather. When he gets angry, red-blue veins show on his forehead and he blows his nose a lot. Grandmother is not as bad as Grandfather, but when I get sick she never comes to my room. I can hear her in the kitchen, asking my aunts whether I am better and when am I going to get up, because the house smells like a graveyard. That's when I cover my head with the pillow and say my prayers to myself, because her words make me feel that my head is about to explode. I begin to hear a buzzing like what comes from the hornets' nest in the patio of the church, and my whole body feels as if it were pricked with hot needles, and then the ceiling falls on the bed in flakes like flower petals or butterfly wings.

# JEWISH CULTURAL CENTER

GREAT PICNIC

On the 29th of June in
MATAMULA WOODS

THERE WILL BE A VARIED PROGRAM OF AMUSEMENTS:
Lotteries, raffles, sack races, three-legged races,
Indian wrestling, pie-eating contest

THERE WILL BE PRIZES FOR ALL

ORCHESTRA FROM 8 A.M. UNTIL 7 P.M.

MODERATELY PRICED BUFFET

If you want to have a beautiful day of fun in the open air,
with your whole family, do not miss this,

ONE OF THE EVENTS OF THE YEAR.

—THE STEERING COMMITTEE

# READERS' FORUM

To the Editor of *Jewish Soul*

Dear Friend:
    As our celebration of Simchath-Torah approaches, I would like to present to you and to all the readers of *Jewish Soul* my opinion of what the program for the celebration should be:

1) Peruvian National Anthem.
2) Jewish National Anthem.
3) Songs and Dances by the children.
4) A one- or two-act comedy acted by adults for children, in which I would like to play a part.
5) A short speech outlining historical and Biblical details that would allow the children to understand the significance of the holiday.
6) A screening of a film on Palestine.

I would only like to add that I am at the service of the Committee whose task it is to organize the program.

Sincerely,

MIRIAM ABRAMOWITZ

# VIII

FROM THE day he met Bertila, Jacobo Lerner began to visit the Wilsons more and more often. Trusting that something profitable would ensue from the relations between the Jew and his daughter, don Efraín had the worn living-room furniture moved to his sons' room and bought a new blue velvet armchair and new wine-red curtains. What had been his exclusive domain was now rearranged for the convenience of the couple.

Only doña Jesús did not participate in the excitement of the house where nothing noteworthy had happened since the time when, during the party that followed Bertila's baptism, Father Chirinos had choked on a chicken bone. "It would be better to use the money to buy a couple of hogs," she said to her husband when he suggested buying a grand piano that a local landowner was selling. His attempts to impress Jacobo Lerner were becoming more and more exaggerated. "Men of the world like don Jacobo are used to being surrounded by refinement. Even though we may be starving, we have to pretend some civility in this pigsty of a house," said don Efraín when his wife tried to show him how ragged his children's clothes were.

For the children, Jacobo Lerner was a legendary character, like the heroes of the adventure films they saw on Saturday afternoons in the town's movie house. They looked upon him as a kind of Count of Monte Cristo, owner of vast shining treasures buried deep in the earth, lord of enchanted palaces in distant kingdoms, consummate swordsman, and tireless traveler destined for prodigious adventures. They never really had direct contact with the mysterious foreigner but watched him through the half-opened door of one of the bedrooms. Early on, Jacobo had discovered the presence of the children and, gladly and faithfully fulfilling the role of story-teller, he played to their interest whenever he visited the Wilson household. All were silent as soon as he came through the door. When he had no more stories, Jacobo would take Bertila on long rides through the outskirts of the village on the bicycle he had asked Edelman to bring from Lima. The acquisition of this vehicle stimulated even further the admiration that Bertila's brothers felt toward Jacobo, in spite of the ferocious criticism that doña Jesús sent in his direction.

Even don Efraín could not avoid the relentless attacks of his wife, who once, after calling him a procurer in the middle of the street and in the hearing of several people, turned her back on him and walked away. Seeing that the problems between them were not going to disappear overnight, and since she refused to cook for him or wash his clothes, don Efraín packed an old, battered suitcase and went to live next door with Pedro and Francisca, his unmarried brother and sister.

Pedro Wilson Rebolledo, a year older than don Efraín, was weak and sickly, with trembling hands and voice. He had a small, wrinkled face more appropriate for an animal from the barren hills than for a human being, and his neck twisted slightly to one side, a consequence, he said, of a blast of cold winter air one night after he had finished drinking a plate of scalding bean soup. Francisca was a crabby old woman of severe brow, incipient moustache, and hooked nose. Whenever she spoke to either of her brothers or her nephews it was to admonish them about Christian morality, or hygiene, or some other social topic. She was, in fact, a fury of a woman who charged against whatever she found in her way, with a single exception: doña Jesús. As far as anyone in the family knew, Francisca had never raised her voice against doña Jesús, because, as she said, "She is an Indian, and with Indians one has to be very careful."

Francisca did not form a very good impression of Jacobo Lerner. Shortly after she met him, she took don Efraín to one side and solemnly intoned that it was "as if they had let the devil into the house." In spite of the fact that his sister's words confirmed the opinion his wife had about the Jew, don Efraín did not waver in his. He spent a restless night, pursued in his dreams by a man with a dark, thin face dominated by blue eyes and a Roman nose. He was wearing tails, top hat, and patent leather shoes, exactly the same way his father had dressed to go to eleven o'clock mass on Sundays. Don Efraín did not know what his dream could mean, but he preferred to think that his father's visit was not of much consequence. Nevertheless, many years later, when Jacobo Lerner was nothing more than a memory, a fleeting ghost that had passed through Chepén, don Efraín would remember Francisca's prophetic words and the dream of that December night.

# IX

## *Miriam Abramowitz: Lima, December 16, 1935*

WILL MY sister come or not?

The truth is I should go see Jacobo, but I don't dare. What if she stands me up, like last time? Well, we have nothing to say to each other and it's best to let things remain as they are. She said she was going to take me to the movies. I'd really like to go, I like Al Jolson, and I spent the whole afternoon looking out the window because yesterday Moisés told me that "we should feel compassion for those who are at the edge of death."

The worst thing is I don't know whether he meant it or not, because sometimes she says something and then she doesn't even show up, so that I wait, wondering where she could be. It would really be funny if Juana had told me the truth.

The truth is Jacobo knows me well, and he should know there are certain things I don't forgive. I don't care if Sara says time cures all. What's that for me? I have to live with my memories.

I could swear Moisés knows nothing.

At what time did she say the movie began?

60

If he knew about it, I can't even think what would happen. I can't even think what would happen if he just suspected what Jacobo was doing. He wouldn't ask me to go see him then, even if he were dying.

Who cares if he is dying?

There was rain last night. Barrels and barrels of rain fell, so that I couldn't sleep the whole night, not even closing all the windows. That smell of damp earth is always there, and when the wood in the furniture cracks I shiver.

I don't know anyone who is sorry. It seems more as if we were getting rid of a heavy weight, like the time Rabbi Weinstein died. He couldn't even open the synagogue any more, and on Yom Kippur they had to go get him from his sickbed. His memory was gone and he fainted in the street.

No one wants to admit it, and I wouldn't say it to anyone's face, but it's the truth.

The time for the movie is past. Moisés is very busy with inventory at the store at this time of the year. Sara says she went to see him, but where could Samuel be? I don't believe the story she told me, that he went to get Jacobo's son. What does he want the boy for now that he's dying? It's better if the boy stays where he is. Moisés says he is not one of ours anymore.

At least the rain cleans the streets. It leaves the stones shining like mirrors.

Samuel ought to come back to make arrangements for the burial. I don't think he's going to bring the boy to Lima. I don't intend to go to the cemetery even if the whole community comes to beg me on their knees, because that would really be the end.

I think Sara's sorrow is all put on. She had a good time a couple of days ago, dancing until I don't know what hour. That was a nice evening, wasn't it? At the end a lot of people came to congratulate me on the program, one of the best we've had in a long time. Kristal was beautiful in her black dress with the décolleté. She said it was brought from Paris, and what a pearl necklace! What a diamond bracelet! But she recites her lines very poorly. Her voice is nasal. Her gestures have no emotion. But even so Sara was envious to see her so radiant. In the

61

middle of the play she went to powder her nose, and she didn't come back until Antonoff began to play the piano.

And all through the dance, not one word of Jacobo's condition. Well, we weren't there to talk about sad things. That would have really disturbed the fabulous atmosphere of the evening. Who wanted to remember Jacobo then and there? He never knew how to earn anyone's love, and only God knows the humiliation and shame he made me suffer.

Not to have the decency to let me know she wasn't coming. What does she think, that I live hanging on what she does or does not do?

I was very careful not to let anyone know of Jacobo's scheming. I kept my mouth shut for my sister's sake, because not even she knew what his plans were. How could she, if she always saw him as the guardian angel of her family? Let her come now and I would tell her. Yes, I would tell her. Why should I keep the secret any longer?

It is nice when the rain cleans the streets. They say the sand is brought by the wind from the desert and it falls all over the city so that in the morning all is covered by it like a white rug, everything white, like a graveyard. It's not like Vienna, always blue. Why is Vienna always blue? Probably because of the Danube; it can't be because of anything else. Well I don't like the smell of damp earth, but it is a good thing when the rain washes away the sand. Lima is like a big hourglass, full of sand, in which time breaks into little pieces.

Sand. In Palestine they are doing marvels. They grow flowers in sand so that the whole country has become a big paradise.

Just now I realize that Jacobo tried to pretend he was innocent and quiet, but beneath the surface . . . always scheming the vilest things that one could imagine. I am not going to tell Moisés he had fallen in love with Sara. Not only that, but more. I told Jacobo once, and I would tell him again if I had the opportunity, because those things should not be asked of a decent woman such as I am. And I was willing to be a good wife to him, but certainly not under those degrading conditions. He didn't find me ragged in the street like he found that Juana. I was poor, yes, but I also had my pride, and I was the mistress of my own life, wasn't I?

That's why I don't care if Sara doesn't come if she doesn't feel like it. I won't cry. That's what they would like. They would like to see the tears that I've held back since Daniel died. But why am I going to start crying like a little girl when I give all of my time and myself to the well-being of the community? Let them, let them see the program I've prepared for this Sunday, all by myself. I've spent hours directing the choir, designing the costumes. And all of that, why? So that everyone can laugh at me behind my back? What do they think? Would it have been better if I had accepted Jacobo's offer? What would they have thought then? I suffered enough when my poor husband died. . . .

Why doesn't this rain stop once and for all?

I am not so stupid that I would fall into the same trap twice. Let them say whatever they want to say. When the time came I knew how to act like a real lady. I don't care if they don't invite me to their houses, and I don't care that they didn't elect me to the Executive Committee of the Ladies' Society, and I don't care about their trips to Europe, and I don't care about their jewels.

She really was beautiful, Kristal. Sara was dying of envy. Well, we never lack for ostentation, but who spends time improving the cultural life of the community? They may do everything at home, yes. They might do everything for their children. But they do nothing for the rest. Only Kristal and a few others participate. That business of giving women's roles to men because the ladies don't want to take part in the plays, that is really the end, isn't it? That's fine for the Japanese but not for us. I've never seen anything more ridiculous. If they were to ask me, I would show them how pleased I would be to take part in a drama. I am not lacking in talent. But, ask me? Let them. I don't repent of anything I've done in my life, and it's been a long time now since I've become resigned to my fate.

Wouldn't it have been a thousand times worse to have married Jacobo Lerner? What I felt for him was not love. All the love I had died with Daniel. Sure, I was ready to respect him and to take care of his house the way a good woman should. But it is impossible to make a home together when all there is is hatred, mistrust, deceit. All very well disguised, that's true, but hatred is still hatred, and deceit, deceit.

What could have become of Sara? I'm not going to wait here for the rest of the afternoon. Does she think I have nothing else to do?

It was raining like this when Jacobo came to propose to me. I was ready for him because Sara had arranged everything and told me so that I had time to settle my thoughts. I had spent the night thinking of Daniel and what he would have said if he had been alive. If he were alive he would have died from it, I think, because for him Jacobo was never anything more than a poor devil. Perhaps he would have understood the situation and accepted the marriage. Who knows? I remember that day as if it were yesterday. I woke up and the sky was very cloudy and I remembered Daniel first thing. Then, for a second only, I saw the sun come out from behind a cloud. I saw it through the window, from my bed, for only a moment, and I became very nostalgic. I remembered all the happy years, and I remembered one day, one summer day, full of sun and of happiness and of desire for life. I remembered Daniel and I wanted to see him again more than I have wanted anything in my life. I wanted to walk with him in a park where the trees were flowering and where all we could hear was the whisper of the breeze in the branches.

But time had broken into little pieces and the rain started to fall, thin and persistent, and I couldn't really hope for anything like that with Jacobo, could I?

Where could Sara be in this rain? I am not going to go looking for her. If that's what she thinks, she's got something else coming.

She even had to tell him how to propose to me, because he had always been a little shy. He came that day all neat and groomed, with a bouquet of roses in his hand. I felt sorry for him, seeing him stammering like a schoolboy because he asked me to be his wife. The truth is I didn't play hard to get, because thinking it over, well, I could see Sara was right, he was a catch.

Of course, I didn't like the way he made his money, but who was I to meddle in his business? He certainly wasn't handsome, except for his eyes. His eyes were black, coal black. And he had no vices. That's important. After all, it was vice that carried my poor husband to the grave, wasn't it? I loved him with all my soul, but that wasn't enough to steer him away from that road. That night, after he had lost all his money playing poker at the Union, he had no alternative but to kill himself.

So he left me buried alive in misery, the laughingstock of the community. What did they say, those vipers, that he put me on the table as a bet? They said that after he had lost the store he wanted to bet me. Why should I pay attention to them? They have always been envious. I know Daniel was never capable of anything so low.

What I can't understand is why Moisés didn't stop him before he had lost the shirt off his back. Moisés called me from the hospital that night, and his explanation was completely incoherent. Nobody could really tell me what had happened. Sara cried all the time we were at the hospital and I don't know why my sister called Jacobo, but he didn't even know the details of the tragedy.

I couldn't recognize his face. It was only a wound, a large wound, so that I returned home with Jacobo feeling that the body I had just left at the hospital was not my husband's, and I spent the whole night waiting for him. Only after dawn did I convince myself that my husband was dead. I still don't understand why his luck was so treacherous to him. He never harmed anyone.

If Sara doesn't come once and for all I'm going to go to the movies by myself.

Who can understand life? He comes to Peru all by himself, he works his fingers to the bone, alone, always a stranger in a new place, why? What for? To die like a dog? There is no justice in this world. That night time broke into little pieces. Pieces, everywhere pieces of time. . . .

Moisés came at noon to take me to the cemetery. There was no one there, we were the only ones, and there wasn't a blade of grass around because he was buried in a spot in the rear of the graveyard. I asked Moisés why the grave wasn't with the others and he put his hand on my shoulder and said, "Don't worry, Miriam, you know how the Rabbi is; we'll see after some time goes by." That's where Daniel rests, even today, all by himself. Sara said his grave is "like a little island."

When we went to uncover the gravestone I didn't see Jacobo until I had walked away on Sara's arm. He came to me to give his condolences again, and his shoes were full of mud. It seemed to me that we had buried him instead of Daniel, and after I had thought that, I felt sorry, because the truth is his eyes were red and he took me all the way home.

If Sara would at least come once and for all! She never comes anymore, because she says she's so busy.

It's not that I am afraid of being alone. That night I learned all about loneliness. I saw the most horrible visions. I saw Daniel's body, rotting. I saw the blood coagulated on his face and I saw the maggots breeding in his body. They crawled out of the box and came into the house through the cracks under the doors and they crawled up the stairs and into my bed, and I tried to get out through the window. It wasn't attempted suicide like my sister said. It was the maggots that had got into my house, so that I had to get out, wasn't it? It was because of the maggots, and because there was no money in the house. After he shot himself there wasn't even enough money to bury him with. At least Moisés paid for the funeral expenses, because if he hadn't I don't know what I could have done. Sell the furniture, perhaps? And what would I have done after that?

To think I almost married Jacobo, no less than Jacobo Lerner! I met him almost at the same time I met Daniel, in the guest house of the Countess. He always wore a checkered shirt and a black cap, and he was so shy he almost never talked to us. Once he talked to me. Once he asked me about Moisés, who was already planning to marry my sister; he asked me whether I knew what he intended to do. He really wasn't very sociable. All he cared about was work. Early in the morning, way before anyone else was awake, he would leave with his case of merchandise, and he wouldn't come back until late at night, dragging his feet and with his head bent. We would gather in the living room and we would dance, or play a few hands of gin, but

66

Jacobo would go straight up to his room and he would stay there.

The truth is I never thought much about his habits, because I wasn't at all interested in him. But at least I didn't mock him all the time the way the others did. I always felt sorry for him. Even now I feel sorry for him, because he is so alone, so abandoned by everyone. But who could have imagined he would open a whorehouse one day? Well, whatever he did with his life is no concern of mine, but what he tried to do with me, that I will never forgive.

He must have made a fortune with that house. Who is he going to leave it to? To Sara? If I were her, I wouldn't touch a penny of it, because tainted money is tainted money. But he will probably leave it to his son. Well, I could use it to get out of the misery in which I live. If it weren't for Moisés . . .

How strange it is that Jacobo is so different from his brother. Moisés is so pleasant, he likes to talk to people, he likes parties. He can spend the whole night dancing polkas and waltzes. They're his favorite dances because they remind him of Minsk.

But my own Daniel had no reason to envy Moisés. He knew how to deal with people better. God, what a talent he had to make me feel like a queen by his side. If he were alive today perhaps he, and not Moisés, would be president of the Union, and I and not my sister would head the Ladies' Society.

It's not that I have anything against Moisés. What little I have I owe him for it. All of us speak of him with gratitude and affection. The truth is I don't understand why Daniel committed suicide. Moisés told me more than once he would have helped him pay his debts, but that fool was always very impulsive. The day my sister got married he appeared in my room and proposed right there and then, and we got married the same day. Everyone was so surprised!

His suicide, too, was a surprise, wasn't it? He left me to the maggots. There were maggots in all colors, green with red polka dots some, and others blue with yellow stripes, and they crawled all together, so close to one another that they seemed to be a carpet on the floor of the house.

The first year of our marriage was beautiful, that I have to say. After the honeymoon he brought me carnations every day. Every week he would take me to the movies, and to dinner in the best restaurants. I never asked him where he was getting the money for such a life. Poor man, his luck only lasted for a year. The day we buried him my sister said to me, "If you had only thought a little you would have realized your husband gambled."

It's five o'clock already. I'm sure she's stood me up again.

Actually, after the first year we stopped going to the movies and we didn't live like rich people as much as before. Daniel had had his store in the Central Market, like Moisés, and I saw that my sister didn't enjoy so many luxuries.

All of this because I followed Sara's advice. Who asked her to meddle in my business? For me Jacobo was always a mystery. Why did he leave Lima the second time? It must be just gossip, evil tongues again, that say he had money problems with Moisés. He came back worse than the way he left, even more closed. The night of the suicide, in the taxi in which he took me home, he said, "Who can believe that things are the way they are?" Who knows what he meant?

The next time we saw each other was in my sister's house. We had a beautiful Seder, but Jacobo said nothing the whole night, as if he were ill at ease, surrounded by strangers and not by his own family. What a strange glow his eyes had! All night he kept them on Moisés, who prayed peacefully in his own house, unaware of his brother's looks of hatred. The same hatred he must have felt toward me when I told him I had decided to cancel our wedding. How was I supposed to imagine what would happen later?

The street is pretty with the lamps lit. The cars go by like comets leaving a trail of red light. Perhaps they called Sara from the hospital?

She made all the arrangements, and after that I began seeing Jacobo every Sunday at their house. It was to please Sara, and for no other reason. It never occurred to me that I might marry Jacobo. What right did she have to try and convince me to marry him?

The truth is at the beginning it didn't seem like a bad idea, but what a man to spend one's life with! He never once took me

68

dancing or to the movies during the whole year in which he was courting me. I used to ask myself, what could this man be thinking? I even considered a couple of times that he might be crazy, once when they put him in the hospital and the other not so long ago when he wanted the whole community to congregate in the synagogue to commemorate the anniversary of the death of a certain Mitrani. Thank God Sara managed to convince him that it wasn't a very good idea! What would people have thought? But madness or not, I guess I was ready to marry him, for convenience, and for no other reason. When Daniel died the community closed all doors for me. And they all spoke behind my back. Who knows what evil things they said?

Not a word about my husband's death, not even a little note in the paper, something to the effect that Daniel Abramowitz's untimely death was regretted sincerely by the community . . . that the community accompanied the remains of a dear friend to his eternal resting place . . . that he leaves behind virtue and goodness that will never fade . . . that he leaves behind a widow in an empty home, a disconsolate woman calling for a husband who will not return. . . .

If it hadn't been for Moisés I would have starved. Not even my father's friends helped me in any way after he died. They would have helped Sara because she stayed to live with him like a dutiful daughter, while I went to live in the guest house run by the Countess. Well, I was grown up, wasn't I?

When my husband died it seemed to me that time had broken into little pieces, and I moved to Jirón Huaraz at the exact moment when all my friends were beginning to buy their own houses. That's why my only hope was Jacobo Lerner.

I didn't realize how things really stood until that woman came to see me. To think the wedding was only a day away when that whore came to put me "up to date." I still feel pain when I remember the horrible things she told me, and no matter how hard I try, I can't forget them.

It's really late now. Sara is not coming, for sure.

She told me, shamelessly, as if there was nothing wrong with it, that Sara and Jacobo had been seeing each other in secret for years, and that he was marrying me to make believe

69

he was marrying my sister. And if that wasn't enough, she told me she, that whore, was his mistress and that they would continue seeing each other after the wedding. Because we, she said "you" and pointed at me and I guess she meant Sara, too, were not real women, we were mannequins to be exhibited with clothes and lace, but not to be taken to bed.

That's not all. She told me Jacobo was going to ask me to take charge of the whorehouse.

How could I have told my sister any of this? I was ashamed even to think of it. When she asked me why I had decided to cancel the wedding I simply told her I was not in love with him, I couldn't do that to Daniel's memory. Daniel had been an exemplary husband, a good man, not someone like Jacobo Lerner who wanted to take advantage of my goodwill.

Well, now that Jacobo is about to die, what is the sense of giving explanations? All that is left for the story to end is for Sara to bring me the news. I'm sure they have taken him to the hospital already, and that's why Sara hasn't come to see me.

If at least Samuel showed some interest in me again, who knows?

To think of what I went through! There were rehearsals for the ceremony. There were a thousand visits to the dress-maker. There were endless conversations with the rabbi on the responsibilities of a Jewish wife. Not to speak of the shame of the ritual bath the day before the wedding. I'm so sorry now I invited the whole community. I am so ashamed of those invitations in black gothic letters with the gold-leaf borders.

Nothing to be done. As soon as Juana left I called Jacobo and told him my decision.

It's getting cooler, so I'd better close the windows. Sara is not coming, for sure.

He begged and he threatened, but nothing could make me change my mind. I even threw him out of the house, actually shoving him. It wasn't until later, when Sara stopped bothering me with her questions and when people stopped talking about it a little, that I had enough peace to think about it and to understand Jacobo's motives.

That's why I told Moisés yesterday that it's better to leave well enough alone.

# X

THE DAY he decided to leave Chepén, Jacobo Lerner stopped
opening the store. He imagined Bertila would keep her pregnancy a secret and that he would have to suffer neither the
flattery of don Efraín nor the anger of doña Jesús. He had
arranged to sell the store to don Manuel Polo Miranda and to
be paid in cash. But before he had made his decision to leave
the village, Jacobo had consulted León Mitrani, who spoke
openly and directly: Jacobo had only two options, he said,
either stay in Chepén, settle down and raise a family, or leave
immediately for Lima, before it was too late.

Mitrani, who didn't want to lose the company of his
friend, favored Jacobo's staying. Jacobo replied coldly that the
idea of marrying Bertila Wilson and staying permanently in
Chepén didn't appeal to him in the least. What he did not say,
perhaps for fear of making Mitrani furious, was that he would
not like to find himself one day in Mitrani's situation: tied to a
superstitious, ignorant woman who had threatened to kill him,
considered a circus freak by the townspeople, abandoned by
those who formerly called themselves his friends, and constantly bothered by the priest to convert.

Jacobo Lerner had come to Chepén with only one goal,
making money, and he was not going to permit blind luck to
make him forego such a practical plan. After his second year in
Chepén, even though his affair with Bertila was already under
way, Jacobo wanted to follow in the footsteps of his brother
Moisés. He wanted to marry a Jewish woman and have many

children. He wanted to live in the capital surrounded by all the luxuries that money could give him. He wanted to go to the synagogue with his friends, to celebrate religious holidays surrounded by his family and to see the bar-mitzvah of his sons. This order of things in his mind was what he leaned on to survive in a country where the way people lived was extremely strange to him. To stay in Chepén now meant giving up all this, to break with the traditional order of his family and his race, in short, to be swirled up in chaos.

"I will die here," Mitrani said when Jacobo proposed they move to Lima together. Jacobo understood then that chaos had already become the master of his friend's spirit, whereas for him, Jacobo told himself in a convincing tone, Chepén was nothing more than a way-station in the travels of his life. He wrote to Moisés telling him he would arrive in July, after he had sold the store.

Don Efraín Wilson had demonstrated great interest in buying the store, but he was not ready to meet the asking price. Jacobo told him that no one would ever become a wealthy man by running a small-town store, which was why he was going to Lima to buy up the government lands next to the mill of Santa Fe and then plant enough sugar cane to supply the mill. He promised to make don Efraín a partner in the enterprise, and he insisted don Efraín keep his plans an absolute secret because the success or failure of the project depended entirely on discretion. Don Efraín swore solemnly, invoking his dead father's name; his lips would be as sealed as a grave.

JACOBO LERNER MET Father Chirinos at the house of Mayor Pablo Morales Santiesteban when a small group of neighbors had gathered to celebrate the mayor's wife's birthday. Jacobo thought Chirinos' appearance corresponded exactly to his profession: he was a tall, thin man with drawn features, and his hands were also long and thin, like those of an old woman of good family. His cassock was always spotless and well starched, his face clean shaven. That night, Father Chirinos spoke in a low and convincing voice about several topics concerning the Old Testament in an attempt to impress Jacobo with his erudition. But the priest's words were replete with mistaken facts and baseless judgments and so did not have the desired effect on Jacobo. Because his father had taught him to respect both civil and religious authority, Jacobo chose not to interrupt while the rest of the guests listened raptly to the priest.

Father Chirinos turned his head this way and that, coquettishly pulled at his sleeves, and at the end of some sentences looked up as if toward the heavens, while an ecstatic expression invaded his face.

The priest stopped only when they began to serve dinner. For Jacobo's benefit, the mayor's wife recited the name of each dish as the serving girl brought them to the table.

Jacobo Lerner had never tasted food like this, because in his hotel he only ordered what appeared to be least harmful to his health and least offensive to his sense of what was proper for a Jew. But now he served himself a little from each dish so as not to slight his hostess. As they ate, they spoke of the climate and the customs of Chepén, of how and when the original clump of houses had been built, and by whom, as well as of the reconstruction of the village after the earthquake of 1920. Mrs. Morales, who came from Chiclayo, told them about that village, larding her conversation with references to one of her ancestors, a Spanish captain who had come to Peru with the troops of Pizarro. When dessert was served, Jacobo was asked to tell something about his life in Russia. And so he related his adventures during the war, describing along the way his own village with its quaint houses and its synagogue, and the Dnieper River, so deep and broad that big barges carried cargoes up and downstream, his father's mill by the side of the river, and the woods nearby which he once had to cross at night in order to evade the patrol. Then he told how he had to sweep streets to earn a living in Germany, and, finally, of how he had arrived in Peru on a rainy night in 1921, on board the steamer *Reina del Pacífico*. He was careful, as he spoke, not to mention León Mitrani's name, judging it unwise to let them know that they had been childhood friends. "I came to Chepén because Samuel Edelman advised me to do so," he said when Father

Chirinos asked him if he had known Mitrani in Russia; "I met León here."

After dinner, the guests sat in the living room. Don Pablo Morales, a short man with bent back and a face that reminded Jacobo of an inquisitive rooster, continued the line of conversation that had been started by Father Chirinos. With the exception of the priest, who had studied in the seminary at Trujillo, don Pablo was considered the most erudite man in the village, and his greatest source of pride was a collection of the classics of Spanish literature. Jacobo Lerner, who had never read anything in Spanish except the newspaper and the catalogues that were essential to his business, was very impressed by the man's conversation, but he did what he could to hide behind his own façade of man-of-the-world. The mayor told about the life of the Jews in Spain during the Middle Ages, of how they had been banished in 1492 by order of the Catholic kings, and of the extraordinary contribution that the *marranos* had made to the political, cultural, and economic life of the nation. "The history of Spain would have been quite different," said don Pablo with an authoritative tone, "if the Jews had not been expelled and persecuted."

Wanting to show that he too had knowledge of what the mayor was talking about, Jacobo added that his teacher in Staraya Ushitza had maintained the selfsame thing, and that he had backed it with statistics, dates, and the names of people and places. The truth was that Jacobo knew little of anything that was not related to the Bible or the Talmud. His acquaintance with history went no further than a few events in Czarist Russia that he had gleaned from Yiddish novels and some discussions with León Mitrani. He could never have imagined that Jews had lived in Spain during the Middle Ages, and he had not the slightest idea of who the Catholic kings might have been or of what the meaning of the word *marrano* was.

"The people of your race always stick together," continued the mayor. "I know that from my own experience. A few years ago, in Chiclayo, I met a certain Mauricio Gleitzer. After another Jew had died, he took the widow and children into his own house. True, I heard later he married her, but that means nothing. What is really important is that instinct all members of your race have. Believe me, don Jacobo, the story I've just told you would never have taken place among Christians. It's not that we don't have the spirit of charity; it's just that we are not as used to helping one another."

After the mayor finished what he had to say, his wife sat at the piano and played "Clair de Lune," one of her favorite pieces, for the guests. Paying scant attention to the music, Jacobo settled in an armchair, and thought of Bertila's pregnancy, of the bent figure of León Mitrani, and of the plans he had made to start a new life in Lima.

# Chronicles: 1925

On the 23rd of July, between ten in the morning and noon, Moisés Lerner moves with his wife and son to a house on Petit Thuoars Avenue.

Jacobo Lerner gets off the bus from Chepén at the Plaza de la Universidad. When he sees his countrymen with their felt hats, their dark coats, and their suitcases full of merchandise, Jacobo remembers his years as a peddler in the capital city. As he crosses the square with long strides, he tells himself that never again, as long as he lives, even if he is sunk in the vilest of miseries, will he engage in that trade. He walks toward the Central Market where his brother Moisés has his store. When he reaches the corner of Abancay and Moquegua, he asks a passerby to show him the way. He goes around the block and stops at the Jirón Huánuco. He walks a half a block more and arrives at his brother's store. The metal gate is down and secured by two enormous padlocks. Jacobo goes into the shop next door to ask about his brother's address. The owner of the store, a fat man with oily eyes, tells him that he has made no mistake, that indeed Moisés Lerner's place of business is the neighboring one, but that it has not been open for more than a week. He does not know what might have happened.

Jacobo goes out into the street, sets the suitcase down, and sits on a bench to wait. He remembers that in his last letter Moisés had told him business could not be better, that he was thinking of opening a ladies' shoestore, and that with the capital Jacobo had saved, it would be very easy to go into business as partners.

Toward noon Jacobo rises, takes his suitcase, and walks toward the Plaza de Armas. Since he doesn't know Moisés' home address, he decides to go to the guest house in Jesús María. He takes the bus on Cuzco Street, and after a ride marked by bumps, jolts, and sharp stops, he gets off at Sinchi Roca Street twenty-five or thirty minutes later. At the end of the block is Madame Chernigov's guest house.

With the help of his wife, Samuel Edelman writes a letter from Chiclayo, addressed to the editor of *Jewish Soul.* The text of the letter is as follows:

Chiclayo, July, 1925

The Editor
*Jewish Soul*

Dear Friend:
Having received the last issue of your magazine, I read with great interest all the articles and even the advertisements. Please imagine my surprise, then, when I saw that many of the strongest Jewish houses of the capital city had failed to advertise.

I confess I did not think it possible that this state of affairs could come to be. These gentlemen transact their business with the rest of the community and depend on it, and for them the cost of an advertisement is a small thing. Is it that they don't realize they have the obligation of supporting a magazine such as *Jewish Soul?* Could it be that they do not understand that gentile merchants, when they realize Jewish firms are not advertising, will conclude they are afraid of spending a few *soles*?

I must tell you all of this is inexplicable to me, and I feel pained and shamed by the actions of some members of the community.

Having nothing more for the moment, I take my leave from you,

Your friend and servant,

SAMUEL EDELMAN

To celebrate Independence Day, the Society of Jewish Ladies holds a ball. The party has a resounding success, and goes on until the early hours of the morning.

# ON JEWS IN PERU

During the last seven or eight years, an enormous number of Jews have come into this Kingdom of Peru through Nueva España, Nuevo Reyno, and Puerto Velo. The city is teeming with them, many married, but most single. They have become the lords of commerce. The street known as the merchants' street is almost wholly theirs.

Elsewhere, they boil through every thoroughfare, selling their merchandise from their cases.

In the market square, most of the stalls are theirs.

In such a way have they become the masters of trade, that everything, from brocade to saddles, and from diamonds to cumin, goes through their hands.

The Spaniard who does not have a Jew as a partner always thinks he is not destined to succeed in trade.

ALFONSO DE ALCAYAGA, 1636

# LITERARY SECTION

In this, his first literary effort, our friend don Mauricio
Gleitzer tries to show a slice in the life of someone newly
arrived in Peru. The author deals with the familiar case of a
cultured and sensitive man as he struggles in a new and
unfamiliar world. We think all the pain and all the suffering are
accurately and artistically reflected.

—THE EDITOR

—Buy, lady, cheap.
—No! Not today!

And the door closes violently in the face of the young
peddler who has a bundle of merchandise on his shoulder.
Silently, depressed by the hostile welcome, he walks away
from the door. The same thing happened to him at the previous
house. Who knows how many doors will be closed to him that
day, in the same fashion? Why this contempt and this hatred?
Is he not human like they are? Doesn't he have a noble and
good heart that lets him feel someone else's pain? Is he not
capable of defending, even with his blood, the soil of this
country? Why, then, do they hold him to be contemptible, a
pariah? Why don't these ladies realize that beneath that shirt,
sometimes dirty, a human heart, deserving of more respect
and more consideration, beats?

Sometimes, during sleepless nights, lying in his bed with
his eyes closed, he thinks of the past: his childhood, the old big
house, the tender loving mother . . . afterward, school, the
fears and uncertainties of examinations . . . afterward, holidays, long walks and picnics with friends . . . afterward, the
last year of his studies, he can now be independent, perfect his
knowledge so that he can become a useful member of society . . . but, cruel destiny! He must emigrate . . . But, good
God! What is happening? Does the man who crosses the ocean

change so much? There he was respected by everyone, and no one fled from his company. And here? So much contempt! So many insults! And he must hold on, accepting everything, in silence . . .

---

JEWISH SOUL: No. 7—July, 1925        **19**

# DR. JULIUS METZKER

## FROM THE UNIVERSITY OF BERLIN

Specialist in lungs, stomach, urinary tract, diseases of the bone, chronic gonorrhea, prostate (cures without surgery), syphilis, and baldness.

### HAS HIS PRACTICE AT

Plateros de San Pedro 161
from 11 to 12 AM
and 5 to 7 PM

# XI

THE COUNTESS opened the door for him. She was dressed in a loose-fitting robe and on her head a red kerchief almost covered her hair, dyed platinum blonde. She had gained a considerable amount of weight since the last time Jacobo had seen her.

Jacobo said a few words in Russian, enough for her to open her arms wide to him as she admitted him into the house. Laughing and exclaiming in surprise, she led him to the parlor where Jacobo noticed the Chinese screen with the birds and yellow flowers artlessly painted on it. He felt slightly uneasy in the semidarkness of the room, and because Madame Chernigov's exaggerated makeup gave her an air both childish and grotesque. Although he was tired and depressed by what had gone on earlier that day, he felt bound to tell her what had happened to him since he had left the guest house in 1923.

When he finished his story, he asked her if she knew where Moisés was living. "The last time I saw your brother was two years ago," answered the Countess, with a deep sigh, "on the day of his wedding." Then, "What can I tell you?" she added. "I have never met a man who was not an ingrate."

Jacobo asked her for a glass of water, and she returned from the kitchen with a bottle of brandy and two glasses. They toasted, among other things, the unfortunate Czar, the unfortunate Russian nobility, and the enchanting Moscow autumns. He noticed that her words, though uttered in a weak tone, had not even a trace of nostalgia. She had arrived in Peru in 1917 and very quickly grown accustomed to her new life. She sold a few jewels she had smuggled out of Russia with her, and with the proceeds had bought the house in Jesús María where she spent several years giving parties, going to concerts, and occasionally visiting a museum. When her money was gone she decided to turn her home into a guest house for Jewish refugees from Russia, who were flooding into the country, according to a friend in the Foreign Office. All she had to do was put a small advertisement in the newspaper and by the following week she had rented all the available rooms. Her first guest was Samuel Edelman who occupied the room next to the garden with a window giving to the street. Shortly after, the brothers Lerner appeared, and they shared a room in the back. The last room she had was taken by Miriam Brener, a girl who had come from Vienna.

With time, all of her guests found different quarters. Samuel Edelman moved a year after he had become a traveling salesman because he preferred to stop at a hotel nearer the center of town whenever he came to Lima to resupply his stock. Jacobo Lerner left one morning in April with his case on his shoulder without telling her where he was going. That same year, Moisés married Sara Brener, whom he had met through her sister Miriam, while Miriam herself married on the same day a friend of Moisés, Daniel Abramowitz, in a double ceremony. "I don't know Miriam's address, either," said the Countess.

Jacobo asked her if she had a room available, and Madame Chernigov took him to the one he had once occupied. Before she left, she informed him that dinner would be served in thirty minutes, at seven o'clock.

As soon as he was alone, Jacobo unpacked his suitcase and carefully arranged his clothes in the drawers of the dresser. Then he lay on the bed and let his eyes roam around the room. A naked lightbulb was hanging from the ceiling; on the night table by the left side of the bed was a roll of toilet paper, several bars of soap, and an ill-used washbasin. He rose from the bed, washed himself quickly, put on a clean shirt, and went down to dinner.

The Countess was in excellent humor during the meal.

She told Jacobo he could stay as long as he wanted, that she was extremely pleased to have a compatriot under her roof. Jacobo, on the other hand, appeared sad and depressed which Madame Chernigov ascribed to the rough trip he had just completed. She had traveled through most of the countries in South America and knew full well what it was to go through inhospitable places in ramshackle vehicles that bounced and jolted on roads that were practically impassable.

Jacobo barely ate, while the Countess, her tongue loosened by wine, recited to him her whole genealogy in strict chronological order, including the story of a pretender to the Russian throne who died, murdered by his mistress, who, in turn, had been poisoned to seal her lips about the crime. Jacobo was surprised that he was the only guest, but that seemed to be the only thing he noticed. He felt dizzy; he didn't know if it was because of the wine or because of the conversation, but he excused himself, bowed shakily, and retired to his room where he took his clothes off and got into bed. For a long time he stayed awake, with his eyes on the ceiling and his hands crossed behind his neck.

What worried him most was the possibility that his brother might have gone, leaving no traces behind. He tried to convince himself that he could put his plans into practice without the help of Moisés. But what really bothered him and what he could not bring himself to admit, was that he could no longer bear his loneliness. The feeling had already begun to bother him in Chepén when he realized he was a man completely unattached, cut off from his traditions, and with absolutely no sense of direction. León Mitrani had at least found some consolation in the religion of his ancestors. Jacobo realized Chepén was already nothing more than a mirage in his memory. Even Lima, though he was there, physically present, began to seem an equally hazy and terrifying landscape.

He remembered when he went to say good-bye to Mitrani in his store the day before he left Chepén. Jacobo had known for a long time that only the slightest threads of the bond that had tied them so intimately in the past remained. From the moment when he decided to leave the village, he had visited Mitrani daily at his house. They sat silently in the orchard as

84

the afternoon light faded, and neither one could think of anything to say. Sometimes Mitrani would stand up and pick the petals off a dying rose, and then he would sit down again, smiling, as if the decadence of his garden were something that pleased him greatly. This state of affairs worsened on the day they first talked about the advantages and disadvantages of staying in Chepén and lasted until the eve of Jacobo's departure. On that night, protected by the semidarkness of the patio, they gave free rein to their emotions and spoke of their childhood. When Jacobo left they embraced with vigor as they had done when they had separated in Hamburg.

As he went out, Jacobo turned and gave his friend one last look. He saw that Mitrani had fallen into his habitual stupor, and that his eyes were vacant.


BERTILA HAD NOT left her house since the night she told Jacobo she was carrying his child. She was the only person in the village who seemed not to know of the Jew's imminent departure. He had not returned to the Wilsons' since he had found out about the pregnancy, and Bertila had not gone to visit him at the store in spite of the entreaties of don Efraín, who could not understand what could have happened to destroy his hope of some day making Jacobo a member of the family.

Doña Jesús, on the other hand, thanked the Lord when she learned of Bertila's decision, raising her eyes to the heavens and crossing herself repeatedly. Perhaps now, she thought, peace would return to the household. Without asking for explanations, she congratulated her daughter for having broken off her relations with the Jew. Eventually, she moved her husband's furniture to the room where it had been before Jacobo's visits and sold the velvet armchair for fifty *soles.* She used this money to buy the couple of pigs that she so desired. She kept them in the pen she had built herself without asking for anyone's help.

The peace that she so ardently wished, however, never came to be, because months after Jacobo had left Chepén,

Bertila found out and was constantly asking about his return. Neither don Efraín's repeated assurances that Jacobo would come back after he had finished his business affairs in Lima, nor the solicitude that her mother showed her had any effect in consoling the girl, who had sworn never to cross the threshold of the house again until Jacobo came on his knees to ask her for forgiveness. Later she threatened to shave her head, cover herself with ashes, and become a nun in a convent.

Since her belly was beginning to show, every morning Bertila would put on a girdle she had made by tearing off some material from the edge of her bed sheet. It wasn't until the fifth month, when the pain this constraint inflicted on her became unbearable, that she exposed her secret, and don Efraín understood at last that the Jew "had given it to him up the ass."

# Chronicles: 1926

Don Moisés Lerner is elected, by unanimous vote, President of the Hebrew Union of Peru.

A year after he opened a shoestore in partnership with his brother Moisés, Jacobo Lerner is swindled by him. Following the advice of Samuel Edelman, Jacobo decides to become a traveling salesman once again. Thus, one morning in August, with his case on his shoulder, he walks to the Plaza de la Universidad, where he boards a bus of the "Roggiero Lines" going north.

Professor Nathan Newman starts a course in Techniques of Breathing and Education of the Vocal Organs (Oratory), which takes place in the Hall of The Philharmonic Society of Lima.

Don Moisés Lerner, President of the Hebrew Union, is the guest of honor at a luncheon given by the Society to express its gratitude for the magnificent way in which he has performed the tasks of his office. In toasting him, don Marcos Kaplan, Treasurer of the Union, makes the following speech:

Ladies and Gentlemen, Mr. Lerner:
It is with the greatest satisfaction that I offer you this modest meal, organized by myself and by all your friends, to demonstrate our deep affection for you because of your work on behalf of the whole community. We were not misguided when we decided upon you to take charge of our destiny, because only a man like yourself, full of enthusiasm and ready for battle, could take the ship of the Hebrew Union to a safe harbor.

Mr. Lerner, I toast you, wishing you and your distinguished family nothing but the best!
I have spoken.


Immediately following, don Moisés Lerner thanks don Marcos Kaplan for his kind words, and the festivities come to an end with a toast for the continued happiness and prosperity of the community.


Jacobo Lerner goes to the commercial establishment of Humberto Martínez, located on Gamarra No. 274, Chimbote, to collect a bill for dress materials he had sold him on the previous day. At first Martínez receives him cordially, but then he changes his tactics and suddenly begins to beat upon the defenseless salesman. Several neighbors are attracted by the noise and they save Mr. Lerner from the fury of his aggressor. Don Jacobo Lerner is admitted to the Chimbote Hospital, where he occupies bed No. 11 in the San Luis Wing.

Federico Lubin and Sara Goldstein, Jewish artists who have recently appeared on the stages of Argentina and Chile, stop in Lima on their way to Havana. Said artists, with the assistance of the amateurs of Lima, currently in the process of reorganization, appear in several dramas in the capital city.

# XII

## *Efraín: Chepén, 1934*

SINCE SHE'S come back from Lima Bertila has been in a bad mood, nagging me all the time because I can't part my hair the way she likes it, because I get the floor wet when I take a bath in the tub, because I lost the scapulary that Grandmother gave me, because I bother everyone with my headaches, because I don't want to go out to play with my friends when I come home from school, because of anything at all. . . . Now she stays in bed until noon and doesn't even have lunch with the rest of us anymore. Instead she goes behind the house and looks straight ahead, as if she were dreaming, and she stays there all afternoon. Grandmother says one of these days they're going to have to drag her to the asylum, where they've locked up Matilde since she lost her son. At night Bertila just disappears. Aunt Francisca says she goes to see the Chang woman, who is a witch and even, she says, a whore, because she cheats on her husband. I've heard it in the village that my Uncle César fucks her. Aunt Francisca says he's always chasing after a skirt, and he has a perfectly straight moustache so with his hair smoothed down he looks like a movie star. He knows how to make a part so that it looks like a white line, without a single wiggle. Grandmother says the Chang woman must have bewitched him, because lately he is very thin, and his face is so sucked in he looks like a skeleton. Grandmother is afraid the same thing is going to happen to Bertila, and tells her again and again not to eat or drink anything when she is in the house of the Chinese woman. Above all, she says, Bertila has to watch out that they don't give her birds' eggs, because they weaken the brain. I think, for sure, Bertila has already eaten them, because she walks around all the time without paying attention to anything. She's fiddling with her hair all day long, and she says it is to clear her head which is full of little crystal balls that bounce inside; and when it isn't that, she is hearing strange noises, the voices of the dead, she says.

All of this since she came back from Lima and she locked herself up with Grandfather so they could talk without my hearing them. But I heard them. "Let's see. What did the Jew tell you?" asked Grandfather. "He told me to go to hell," she answered him. Grandfather got very angry. "What do you mean, he sent you to hell? And his son?" he shouted. "He doesn't want him in Lima," Bertila said. "He said it would be better if he stayed here in Chepén, with me. He's going to keep sending money as long as we keep him here."

I heard nothing but footsteps for a while, then again, Grandfather's voice. "What did you tell him?" he asked. "I told him if he didn't take the boy I was going to go to the police," Bertila said.

"Good," said Grandfather. "Good. What did he say?" I think Bertila was crying, but I'm not sure. "That if I kept bothering him, the next time I came to him with threats he was going to call the police himself and he was going to have them lock me up." "Jesus Christ!" shouted Grandfather, "that bastard has a pair of balls the size of . . . of . . . and if we sent the boy to live with Mitrani?"

I didn't get to hear what Bertila answered because I began to itch everywhere as soon as I heard Mitrani's name. Grandmother says he is the devil disguised as a storekeeper. The truth is he didn't do anything to me that day when Ricardo convinced me to go to his house to scare his wife. She's an old woman who never goes out into the street because she is blind. First we had to jump the fence, and then, as we were sneaking through the orchard, I got a thorn in my heel. Ricardo had to get it out with his teeth, because he couldn't do it with his nails, which are all chewed up. I can't bite my nails because if Aunt Francisca finds out she smears my fingers with shit, so that they stink and I can't put them in my mouth. Then we went through a window, slowly, because my foot hurt and I told Ricardo I could hardly walk. If we don't leave, I told him, I will faint right here and you'll have to carry me home on your back. "Don't shit in your pants, Efraín," he said. "Wait just a little longer. We're almost in the old lady's room. We only have to go up the stairs. Be careful. Some of the boards are loose."

"It's better if we go back, Ricardo," I said. "If the old man gets his hands on us he might eat us alive."

"Don't be such a baby," he said. "The old man is in the store at this time every day. We're there. See? Her room is at the end of this little hallway."

The door was half-open and we went in without making any noise. The old woman was lying on the bed like a dead body. She had large feet and very hairy legs, like a monkey. Her waist was as thick as the barrels in which Chang keeps his olives. We hid behind a dresser, I don't know why, because the old lady can't see anything and we started to howl quietly, like souls in purgatory. But the old lady sat up on the bed without being at all frightened and moved her head from side to side as if to hear better. Her hair was all tangled up, it looked as if she never combed it. She got up a little higher, leaning on her elbows, and asked with a shaky voice whether it was her sister who had come to visit her. That's when my teeth started to chatter and I got goose bumps all over. But I was also giggling because Ricardo started to lead her on with a soft voice like the voice of the dead who return from the grave. "Herminia," he said, "Herminia, listen to me. I am your sister Ernestina. I am your sister Ernestina, and I have come to give you bad news."

The old lady opened her mouth wide and craned her neck, stretching to hear better. "Sister," she said, "where are you, sister? Come closer so that I can feel you."

"You can't touch souls, sister," said Ricardo. "Stay where you are and listen to me well, because I can't stay long."

"Yes, sister. Yes. Tell me, sister," said the old lady. Ricardo put on a voice as if he were crying and said, "Herminia, our father died last night. Doctor Meneses stuck an enema up his ass and blew out his guts."

Then the old lady began to scream in such a way that we ran out of the room as if the house were on fire, and suddenly a hand picked me up by the neck and dragged me back to the old lady's room like a bundle. I heard the voice of old man Mitrani. "Calm down, calm down, woman. It's only Jacobo's son."

But the old lady was half-hysterical. "León," she shouted. "My father died last night. The funeral must be now, in his house."

"You are mad!" said Mitrani, very angry. "Your father died a long time ago. Doctor Meneses killed him."

Now I really was going to get it. I hoped Ricardo had gone straight home to get Bertila, because the old man took me down to the living room which was very dark even though it was the middle of the day. The only light came from seven candles almost guttered down in a strange candle holder with seven arms and flowers and leaves of metal that twisted like the flames of the candles and deer with thin little horns that looked like spaghetti. Old man Mitrani forced me to sit on a chair and began to look at me very carefully, with his hand on his chin. "You look just like your father," he said to me. "You have the same eyes, the same nose, and those big, big ears. All one has to do is look at you and one can tell you are one of ours."

I had my eyes wide open, waiting for the old man to swallow me. I couldn't say anything because my mouth was so dry.

"Your father and I were very good friends," he went on. "We grew up together, like brothers . . . but he had to leave for Lima. That was eight years ago, before you were born. But he loves you very much, and you'll see that some day he is going to come and get you because he will never forget about you."

I didn't make very much sense of what he said because all I wanted was to get out of there as quickly as I could, and suddenly somebody knocked on the door. It was Aunt Fran-

93

cisca, and she came in with a shining crucifix in her hand, holding it like a sword. "Let the boy go or I am going to get a policeman," she shouted at Mitrani.

"What's the matter with this old scarecrow?" he said. "Can't she see that I'm not doing anything to the boy?"

But Aunt Francisca ran into the living room and dragged me out to the street.

"You old witch! You old witch!" shouted Mitrani from the door. "Stick your crucifix up your ass! It's high time the boy is told who his father is!"

# Chronicles: 1927-1929

Jacobo Lerner spends a restless night in a hotel at San Pedro de Lloc, a small town about fifty kilometers from Chepén. He wakes up before dawn, turns on the lamp on the night table, takes pencil and paper, and begins to write a letter.

San Pedro, November 15, 1927

The Editor
*Jewish Soul*

Dear Sir:
Allow me to answer the letter of Mr. Samuel Edelman, who some weeks back wrote of his favorable views on the integration of Jews in Peru. Without wishing to offend Mr. Edelman, who is a good man, I think that the assimilation that threatens us is like a terrible octopus. Its tentacles take in all the members of our community, our children, our young people.

If those who become assimilated participate fully in Peruvian life, adopting some Peruvian customs but remaining Jews in spirit, religion, and tradition, there is no harm. We are, after all, Peruvian Jews. Unfortunately, there are many among us

95

who have married women of another religion; there is no room in their homes for the Jewish spirit, and they educate their children outside the Jewish tradition.

There are others who prefer, because of fear or shame, to say that they are German, Russian, French, Austrian, etc., and deny strongly that they are Jews.

These are the forms of assimilation that we must all fight.

Sincerely,

JACOBO LERNER

A matinée for children takes place on Sunday, November 23, in the main hall of the Hebrew Union. The attendance is most impressive, since the room is filled to capacity by members of the community. The Ladies' Group prepares a beautiful lunch in the adjoining hall. An interesting touch is added by the large number of Sephardic families who, apparently following the general enthusiasm, visit the Union for the first time.

At 4:00 P.M., don Moisés Lerner, acting in his capacity as President, opens the ceremonies with a brief speech in which he refers to the reason for the gathering and its meaning to the children. He is vigorously applauded.

Immediately afterward, the children's choir sings both the Hebrew and the Peruvian national anthems, accompanied by Miriam Ackerman, nine years old, on the piano.

Jorge Alcabés, twelve years old, follows, reciting the poem "I am a Little Sephardic Child." Then Marcos Roitman, thirteen, recites "Main Rebe."

Miriam Ackerman returns to play a waltz on the piano.

Paulina Kalman, ten years old, recites "My Little Doll."

Simón Ludmir, thirteen, recites "Hatzipor" by Bialik.

Rosita Rosenblat, twelve, recites the poem, "My Mother."

Finally, José Osc, seven years old, closes the first part of the program with the poem "A Mother's Advice."

Following this, the winners of the chess championship receive their medals from Miss Berta Rosen, sponsor of the tournament. Each is received with enthusiastic applause. The second part of the program begins with "Hatikva," played on the piano, four hands, by Ackerman and Kalman. The brothers Ludmir then sing "Zug mir rebenim." Paulina Kalman sings and dances "Under the Rain." The choir puts an end to the afternoon by singing "Hatikva."

In Pacasmayo, Jacobo Lerner gets to know Abraham Singer, a Polish Jew about fifty years old. Singer impresses Jacobo as an unusual man. What hair he has left surrounds his bald pate like a half-moon; he is less than five feet tall; his legs are bowed; he walks with short, springy steps, swaying from side to side. But what Jacobo finds most remarkable about his friend is his occupation.

Abraham Singer is the owner of "The Caravan of Pleasure" and earns his living by providing women to the military garrisons of the north. However, his business is not restricted to soldiers. Occasionally he will set up his tent in one village or another, having already bribed the mayor and the chief of police with a percentage of his earnings.

When Jacobo asks him why he is involved in such a disreputable, not to say dangerous, business, he adopts a dignified pose and delivers a speech about complying with patriotic duty. Besides, he adds, there are altogether too many Jewish merchants in the region, and sooner or later there will be a catastrophe. He has seen, as he travels all around the north, that in some villages they have begun to accuse Jewish traveling salesmen of being Communist agitators. He concludes that in times such as these it is far better to let people believe he is Turkish and not Jewish.

Since Jacobo has to go to Ferreñafe, too, he decides to go with the caravan.

After they have been on the road for half an hour, Singer

97

tells him that he thinks he will stop at Chepén, where he will set up his tent for a few days.

Shortly before they come to Chepén, Jacobo tells Singer he will not be able to accompany him any further, since he has to take care of urgent personal business elsewhere.

Jacobo Lerner sits by the side of the road, waiting for the bus that will take him farther north, directly to Ferreñafe. In the distance he sees soldiers approaching on trucks.

He picks up his suitcase, crosses the highway, and manages to hide, out of breath, behind a hill. When he can no longer hear the noise of the trucks he leaves his hiding place. He crosses the highway again, sets his suitcase down, and with trembling hands he takes a handkerchief from his pants' pocket and slowly wipes the sweat off his face.

He thinks of León Mitrani, of Bertila, and of the son he does not know. He decides that as soon as he finishes collecting what is due to him in Ferreñafe he will return directly to Lima.


Don Augusto B. Leguía is reelected President of the Republic.


From Chiclayo, Samuel Edelman sends the following letter to the Editor of *Jewish Soul*:

Chiclayo, December 22, 1928

The Editor
*Jewish Soul*

Dear Friend:

A few days ago, the Lima newspapers published a report of the COMMITTEE FOR SOCIAL DEFENSE, in which it was said that Jewish traveling salesmen spread Communist doctrine and that they must be fought without quarter.

In view of this new slander, and in view that it might severely damage our concerns, because we are only interested in earning an honest living, I hope the Syndicate of Traveling Salesmen will come to our defense, denying the allegations of the COMMITTEE.

Sincerely yours,

SAMUEL EDELMAN

Jacobo Lerner returns to Lima on a Saturday morning and stays at the house of Marcos Geller. Marcos gives him a letter from León Mitrani that Edelman had delivered. For two weeks, Jacobo carries the letter in his pocket without daring to open it. When he finally decides to read his friend's letter, Jacobo turns the envelope in his hands thinking of the efforts he has made to banish the memory of León, only to have him constantly reappear in his dreams. Sometimes he is there with a prayerbook under his arm, walking in the courtyard of Rabbi Finkelstein's school. At other times he is shrouded in the thick smoke from the chimney of the ship in which he had sailed, without lights and to no port.
This is the letter from León Mitrani:

Chepén, August 15, 1929

Dear Friend:
This is not the moment to speak of certain things that belong to the past, but I remember I once warned you it is not easy to find the peace and happiness that one wants so badly. Nevertheless, you still have time to begin again. I chose to be tranquil and peaceful, and you should follow my example.
Your wife and son are waiting anxiously for you in this village. If you return to Chepén you will be rich in a very short time.
Your friend who loves you and misses you,

LEON

# PEOPLE OF THE INQUISITION

(Exclusive for *Jewish Soul*)

**DIEGO NUNEZ:**

Born in Travira, he denounced himself in March, 1570, for having said that Jesus Christ went to Limbo both as man and as the son of God. He was condemned to say a Mass in the Cathedral, to having his sentence publicly read, and to repent from his heretical statements.

**ARIAS BELLO:**

Born in Algarbe, he too denounced himself for blasphemy. He was condemned to pay for masses for the conversion of the Indians.

**MANUEL DUENAS:**

He was condemned in this city to spend the rest of his life in the Hospital de los Marineros. Further, he had to hear the mass and sermon at the Cathedral every Sunday. Further, every Saturday, he had to go on pilgrimage to the church of La Merced, where he had to confess and receive the sacrament on the four main holidays. He died insane.

> FRAY FERNANDO,
> Lay Brother of the Convent
> of La Merced

# ATTENTION

MEMBERS OF THE COMMUNITY:

The time has passed when one came to this country to make money and then returned to the country of one's birth. Today, when we come to a South American country, we come with the full intention of making it our permanent home. Therefore, we must adopt the citizenship of the nation that so generously opens its doors to us.

BECOME A NATURALIZED PERUVIAN CITIZEN!

# NEWS OF THE COMMUNITY

## ACCIDENT

Don Jacobo Lerner, traveling salesman, was run over by a car as he crossed Alfonso Ugarte Avenue. He was taken to the emergency ward of the Public Hospital. Though his injuries were not minor, he was allowed to go home after he was treated.

## THE CASE OF THE "DOCTOR"

Our readers know well how a certain person arrived in Lima about four years ago claiming he was a medical doctor, and how, after gaining the confidence of many members of the community, he made them victims of his crime.

After defrauding his patients and a few commercial establishments, "Doctor" Julius Metzker disappeared from Lima. He was arrested by the police in Pacasmayo, and then returned here. Soon after, he managed his release and went north, where he tried to repeat his schemes. Fortunately, members of the community saw through him in time.

For several months now we have not heard of the good "doctor," and we were beginning to think that we never would again. A few days ago, however, we learned through the local press that the "doctor" had been arrested in Trujillo and sent back to Lima on the request of the authorities here, where he still has a few accounts to settle with members of the community.

# LITERARY SECTION

## COUNTRY WALK

So it is that having lived in contact with nature for but a few hours interrupted the ordinary flow of my existence and has made me sing of life with my whole being. . . .
One morning the sun beat down mercilessly but at the same time a clear breeze cooled the air. My friends and I fled the confines of the city to take refuge in the freedom of the fields. Never before had I perceived the smell of the earth and the flowers with such intensity, and never before had I felt the simple joy of living as strongly as I did that day.

It is true that with our voices we disturbed the calm silence that reigned there. We frightened a little the trees that were dancing to the rhythm of the breeze, and even the birds that were singing their song.

It is true that we ran through the fields, forgetting ourselves, jumping fences as we danced, and interrupting the afternoon sleep of the insects in their soft bed of fallen leaves.

But it is also true that the countryside forgave us all that, because there we became what we really are and are afraid to show in the city: people full of joy who need to express it some time or another.

Then we realized that the shadows of the afternoon had fallen, and it was necessary to go back.

As soon as we came into the city we began again to fill the roles we fill every day, but we said good-bye sure of having lived life in a better, pleasanter way.

This is something we should do more often. It would strengthen our bodies and it would raise our spirits. It would allow us to walk through life serenely.

SARA LERNER

## DREAMED BY JACOBO LERNER
## ON THE NIGHT OF SEPTEMBER 25, 1929

Gray gray   everywhere gray
gray gorge   gray rocks   gray hands
gray sword
sure and cutting   blood head crown
gray hands            stumps growing
sword thrusts         voices gray
*Vi Got iz dir lib los undt nisht iber!*

drizzle fine blood red        wind
gray rocks
sinking blood red
León eating bones
Yankel your father has just died
hand in hand longtime
gray round of birds
river-bank
*river-bank Ich ken nicht ariber tsu yener*
       *zait*
burying hands
stump on the helm
*di gantse Zait?*   Looking looking Judit
mothers and children mothers and children
long line
blood
laughing
gray                      gray
barbed wire               pines
dogs                      pines
gray guards               gray
door                      white house
snow                      white snow
hair                      white hair
why have you come?
*Gud du bist gekumen*
mother voice
*is ersht Itst geshtorben*
body burial snow

gray ship
wrinkled hands gray
thrusts
new
running
*Los unds nisht iber Yankel*

gray voices unknown
ship
woman
gray birds
*Gud du bist gekumen*
León on his feet
walking
night
gray ship

face
gray soldier
*Mishka vu bistu geven*
river-bank
stop Mishka stop
handless helmsman
singing
water
water
guns
gray
pines
white gray house
white gray snow
white gray hair
your father has just died
suitcase shoulder
*Dain tate*
again
white gray hair

gray body
black coat white hat
father father father father father father
gallop gray gallop
pines
patrol
dogs
gray gorge gray rocks
sword thrusts
*Farlos ins nit Yankel*
blood
blood
closed eyes
woman

melting
the road
father father
melting white gray snow
barbed wire
gun
gray ship
stump
sure cutting
drizzle
river
gray ship
turned heads
the ashen coast

# XIII

## *Efraín: Chepén, 1934*

THE GYPSIES are all over town. They've made a whole village of tents just outside and then they come in, going from house to house. The other day I answered the door and there was an old gypsy woman who just stared at me with her mouth open, showing her gold teeth. I called Bertila, and the old woman said to her, "Are you the mother of this boy?" "Yes," Bertila answered, "I am. What do you want here?" And the woman spoke with her golden teeth. "How much do you want for the boy, miss?" Bertila opened her eyes wide and looked at me and I crouched and grabbed her by the legs because she smiled and asked, "How much will you give me?" "You, miss, you tell me how much you want," the gypsy said. "What would you say to a hundred *soles*?" said Bertila, and I let go of her legs and ran out to the courtyard as fast as I could, almost choking, and no matter how far away I got from the house I could still hear her laughing in the living room. That night I dreamed Bertila sold me to the gypsies and the old woman took me with her on a long journey to a cave under a lake where there was a tall dark man with eyes like coals, and he opened his arms and called me son, and everyone knew that he was the king of the gypsies. Then I woke up, and I wasn't even sweating, and I didn't even have chills, I felt all right, and in my chest there was a calm, ease . . .

It's been a while since Ricardo and I have been to school. Not even Aunt Francisca says anything if I spend the whole day swimming in the river, or walking in the fields. I don't like to stay in the house anymore, seeing Grandmother at the door of the kitchen, crushing lice. It's not like it was before, when Aunt Francisca would beat me with a belt if I didn't go to school. Now she only cares about Iris. She has Iris living with her in the house, so that nobody will bother her. Iris isn't allowed to go out anymore, because as soon as she was well Zoila started shouting insults at her, and told her that because of what she had done she would never be able to marry her druggist and would be a spinster for the rest of her life, like Francisca, and like Bertila.

I have exactly one *sol,* and this afternoon I'm going to go to the movies no matter what. I would never get to set foot inside the "Alfa" if it weren't for don Fermín, who buys old nails from me. Since it's Easter week, this afternoon they're going to show a religious movie. Aunt Francisca says that it is silent and that the actors make gestures and move their mouth as if they were speaking, but they don't say anything. Bertila sometimes does that. Father Chirinos says the movie is very sad and you've got to have a heart of stone if you don't cry, but Grandfather says he has seen it and it is very funny, and asked who the hell was going to cry at that kid stuff.

I don't know who to believe. I used to love Father Chirinos a lot. Aunt Francisca says that he favored me from the day of my christening. The first time I went to confession I was so nervous I thought I would die, but Father Chirinos caressed my head and smiled at me, and I smiled back until I wasn't afraid any longer. Ricardo had told me that you have to undress during confession to show your sins to the Father. I didn't know whether I had any, though Aunt Francisca had told me no one is free of sin because the devil is everywhere and we can't see him because he is full of tricks and sometimes he even turns into air. Aunt Francisca says he gets into all of our bodies, even those of children, and makes us do dirty things. After confession Father Chirinos gave me an image of Saint Rosa and I took it home to put it under my pillow. I used to go to church every afternoon then. From the altar I could see Jesus Christ up close, and I could also see the Virgin with the baby in her arms. He looked like a little doll and Aunt Francisca told me he was the child Jesus and that when he grew up he died on the cross where the Jews had nailed him.

That's why I loved Father Chirinos a lot then, because he taught me how to read and because he knew a lot of stories about the first Christians in the world and how they suffered because they believed in Jesus Christ. They were chased and killed by men with shields and swords and strange helmets. He also told me how Jesus Christ had come to the world to save us, the Christians, and how after he was crucified he came back to life again and went to heaven with his Father. Bertila didn't like to hear me speak of these things. She used to say that Jesus was a horse's ass who let himself be killed just because. Whenever that happened Aunt Francisca would tell me not to pay attention to Bertila, that she had gone mad because of suffering. But I used to go to the church then, and stayed a long time looking at Jesus Christ and then Father Chirinos and I used to pray an Our Father together in a low voice.

Until after a while he didn't love me anymore and never called me "son" again. I think he began not to like me one day when I told him I didn't believe in Jesus Christ anymore, to see what would happen. I saw that he lifted his hand to slap me and I got so frightened I knelt in front of him and begged him to forgive me. But he didn't smile or anything, and since then he hasn't been the way he was before. When he sees me in church now he doesn't speak to me and even goes to his room so he doesn't have to see me. Yesterday I followed him there, and when I opened the door I saw him sitting on the bed with his face in his hands. The room was so empty without even a chair, and standing there I asked him who my father was. "What kind of a question is that?" he said. "Jesus Christ is your father." But I told him that I wanted to know about my real father. "Your real father, your only father, is Jesus Christ," he said slowly.

Aunt Francisca told me my real father died nine years ago in a fire at his store, I insisted. Father Chirinos admitted this was true. I wanted to know where he was buried. "We didn't bury him here," he said, after thinking a while. "We sent the body to Lima because old man Mitrani was set on it."

"But Mr. Mitrani says that my father is alive in Lima," I went on. "You know Mr. Mitrani is crazy. How can you pay attention to what he says?" Father Chirinos answered.

"Well, then, is it true that my father was a Jew like Mr. Mitrani?"

"I only know that he didn't believe in our Lord Jesus Christ, as every good Christian should."

"Is it true that the Jews killed Christ?"

"Yes. They tormented him on the cross, without mercy, until he died."

Then I ran crying out of his room and out of the church, and I was still crying when I got home. I couldn't sleep all night thinking of what Father Chirinos had said, and in the morning I asked my grandfather who my father had been, and like other times he told me not to bother him with silly-ass things. Didn't I see he was taking inventory?

Well, I am not going to go to Mr. Mitrani's store, even though he says my father is living in Lima, because if I do Aunt Francisca is capable of cutting my ears off. I can't ask my Grandmother anything, I can't even talk to her as she sits crushing the lice because she seems to be very far away. But this afternoon I am going to see it with my own eyes, because the movie they are going to show at the "Alfa" is called "Life, Passion, and Death of Our Lord Jesus Christ."

# XIV

## *Sara Lerner: Lima,*
## *December 16, 1935*

WHAT TO do? I can't make decisions, that's my problem. All my friends keep telling me "Make up your mind once and for all, Sara. We don't even have the program yet." I know. I know. But it makes me angry when they tell me. Because, who is it that works the hardest? You either do things well or you don't do them at all. You just can't put on anything tasteless so that it's done. That's the way it was with the Kauffman woman. She should have stayed in the kitchen, peeling potatoes, not become the president of the ladies auxiliary. They got used to her. But the responsibility is mine now. Mine and no one else's.

I told Jacobo you have to learn to deal with both failure and success, that is a virtue. I don't blame anyone else when things don't turn out the way I plan them. That's why I have to plan them well. But does he pay attention to what I tell him?

I could stay home all afternoon reading magazines, if I wanted. It says here that "objects made of shell take on a beautiful shine if one rubs them with a soft cloth." But I could also go see Miriam. Yosef is in school and the maid will make his dinner. Moisés is not coming home until late. "Another use for a soft cloth is to rub a slight amount of shoe polish on old records. That way it is possible to smooth over some of the scratches."

Moisés doesn't like it when I spend the whole day outside the house. But it's not my fault. I have my obligations too. If I don't do these things, who is going to do them? I can't just stay home and cook for him all day. I would go crazy. I have my life too.

My life is better than other lives, I'm sure of that. All I have to do is look at Miriam and I know how lucky I am. Was it better in Vienna? I don't know. There's no comparison between Vienna and Lima. There are so many people without culture here, and the streets are always dirty. Sometimes I feel like going back to Europe. Yes, and all that is going on in Germany? Besides, who is going to get Moisés out of here?

Jacobo would take me if I asked him.

A long trip on a ship, that's what I need to get out of this routine. "A little pork fat can be used very well to clean black velvet."

I still have to make all the arrangements for the fair next week. Thank God the performance for this Sunday is already organized, because if it weren't . . . When Miriam finds out we have changed the program from beginning to end she is going to have an attack. After all, the way she wanted it was not too . . . I don't know how to put it. Everyone agreed.

I don't know why I agreed to go to the movies with Miriam if I really don't want to go. Because I feel sorry for her? I would really have to be a fool to go out in this rain. Rain, rain, it's been raining since yesterday. It is a sad rain. In Vienna the rain is gayer, it seems to sing.

Moisés says that his corns hurt. They always do when it rains at night. Of course, I had to get up to warm some water for him, cold as it was in this house. They said on the radio it's going to rain all day tomorrow, again. I hope it doesn't rain on Sunday, because the fair is going to be outdoors.

I won't be able to go to Jacobo's house. I didn't promise

him I would go or anything, but I told Moisés that after all, Jacobo was his brother. All he said was I could do what I wanted.

Every time I speak to him about Jacobo he gets angry and doesn't talk to me for the rest of the day. It's better to leave him alone, though I don't know what it is that he has against his brother. Where would he be if it hadn't been for him? And Jacobo doesn't harm anyone except for his business. That makes the whole community look bad.

Why did Jacobo love me?

If he dies on us now, good-bye to the fair. How am I going to go see him alone? If Miriam came with me it would be a different story. "Mr. and Mrs. Hellman gave a party on the occasion of Mrs. Fishman's departure for Europe."

What to do? I can't go and ask her, just like that, say Miriam, let's go see how Jacobo is. She would throw something at me, and I wouldn't blame her. Actually, I would like to see her expression if I asked her. "Mr. and Mrs. Katz, Mr. and Mrs. Lerner, Mr. and Mrs. Brener, Mr. and Mrs. Kaplan were all there." I'm sure that she is stewing because she wasn't invited. Good God, the lies she tells. Who doesn't know that it was Jacobo who canceled the wedding at the last moment and not her?

Imagine that, coming to tell me she did not want to marry Jacobo, as if I could believe her. Lying to me, who knows her better than I know the palm of my hand. She should have given thanks to God about the wedding. Who else would have her? At forty we can't afford to be choosey, that's what I told her. "More people travel on Goodyear tires than on any other brand."

Choice? Of course she had no choice. She should have been grateful that I arranged everything. It's time you settled down, I told Jacobo. Where are you going to find a better woman than Miriam? What you need is a Jewish home.

He did it for me, and only for me. I'm the only one he listens to. He pays attention to no one else. If it hadn't been for me he wouldn't even have gone to the hospital.

Anyway, he was the one who canceled the wedding. God knows why he changed his mind at the last minute. He didn't say anything to me, and I had to cancel the ceremony. It would have been beautiful. We were going to decorate the main ballroom at the Union with flowers. Not like when I got married, when we didn't have flowers or anything. But that was years ago, and things have certainly changed since then. "Italia, the best company for all your insurance needs." Have they gotten better? Yes. But the rumors that are circulating around the community are really something. Poor Miriam. She hasn't been the same since Daniel died. She even tried to kill herself, throw herself out of the window. Thank God they stopped her in time, because if not that would really have been a scandal.

She is a luckless woman, that's what she is. If it weren't for Jacobo she would be in the street. She thinks the money comes from Moisés, as if we could afford it, with all the expenses we have. We aren't as rich as she imagines we are. Don't tell her, Moisés says, let her believe whatever she wants. And Jacobo doesn't want her to know, because he thinks she wouldn't take the money if she knew it was coming from him.

What's going to happen now that Jacobo is dying? We'll see. I can't allow my sister to be thrown out into the street with no place to go. Of course Moisés won't have her here. But if Jacobo's son comes to live with us, then we could send her some money and Moisés wouldn't say anything because it would still be coming from Jacobo, in a way.

I wonder how much money Jacobo has in the bank. It must be a fortune, what with the new business in La Victoria. Moisés says that he should have done the same thing. But I don't care how much money Jacobo makes, I wouldn't let Moisés do anything like that. I mean, he is the President of the Union and all—what would the community say?

He has enough troubles already explaining about his brother, who has stained their parents' name. He doesn't even want to think that a few years ago Jacobo saved him from bankruptcy. He would be in jail if it hadn't been for Jacobo, and I would be in the streets, with my son.

All right, I owe Jacobo everything, and I wouldn't exchange my happiness for anything in the world. I told him. I told Jacobo.

Who knows whether he really loved me? Poor man, he is so alone it makes me feel sorry. He deserves better luck than he has had. But, after all, he owes me a lot too. I am not an ingrate, but I also had no obligation to invite him to my house and to make him part of the family.

No one forced me to go see him in the hospital. I was the only one, too. All his friends have abandoned him. I don't blame them, either. I was afraid to go see him, because I read somewhere that madness is contagious.

I wonder whether he is really mad. Poor man. He just lay there, as if he were asleep, without saying anything. What could he have been dreaming about with his eyes open? I always dream of my parents' house in Vienna, my bedroom and my dolls. Mother died when I was very little. I didn't know anything about her life, and I hardly remember her. Maybe Miriam remembers her. No. I'm sure that Jacobo wasn't dreaming. How could he dream if he is crazy? Do crazy people dream?

Crazy. Everything he said was the truth. Why couldn't it happen in Peru? I get goose bumps when I think of things that have happened here before. Barbarians, to kill and torture people just because they were of another religion. Moisés says times change and we are safe here. But what's happening in Germany? Who can tell the same thing is not going to happen here?

I don't care what they say, I don't trust the goyim, not even in Lima. The newspapers are always so full of slanders, it's clear they hate us as hard as they can.

What can I do now? I can't go visit him if I have nothing to tell him. It would be better if I went by Miriam's house. It might be easier if we went together.

I am sick of seeing people die. Death, death, and death, as if we had a curse on our heads . . .

The literary page is always good. "I remember that night. The moon was shining in a dark blue sky, surrounded by stars that spilled their light on the fields." When father died Miriam didn't even come to the house and left me to take care of him and even to make arrangements for the funeral. I had to take a basin of water and bathe him in his bed, and he smelled of death even before he died. Then I had to see Daniel with his face blown off. "We walked in the garden flowering with May." I cried in the hospital, but it was only because I was afraid. It could have been Moisés who shot himself, because he had lost quite a lot of money too. Good Jacobo again, rescuing him from ruin. "We breathed the perfumed air of the balmy evening." He never complained. Never even said anything about what Moisés had done to him. I don't even want to remember. These things belong to the past.

What can I do, then? I really don't dare go alone. It would be different if Miriam came along. I can't try to convince Moisés to come because I know how busy he is with the store. That and his duties as president. It takes more than a little time to do things right. The community would be nowhere without him. Thank God, everyone appreciates what he does. Who remembers Jacobo? With all his time and money he's never done anything for the community.

It's not easy to do these things when you have a family. If it were only up to Moisés, we would already have a new synagogue. I'd better get busy with dinner; he's coming home at eight o'clock, and he will want it ready. I've got a lot of obligations, but he wants a Jewish home such as a Jewish home should be, and on Friday evenings I light candles and everything. Where does it leave me, a modern woman? I'm going to cook him a chicken. He has to take care of himself, I tell him. Doctor Rabinowitz is right when he says that one must always eat at the same time. He has to rest, I tell him. It's impossible to work all the time and be healthy. But he is the way he is, and he takes his duty to the community seriously, and at least they recognize his efforts and appreciate him. Which is the way it should be, not the way things are with Jacobo. I am even ashamed to hear his name sometimes. People sometimes speak of his business on purpose, so that I can hear them.

It must be a very strange world. I can't even imagine him the way it is in the movies, with those red lights and the half-naked women. Could it be true that he was going to ask Miriam to . . . ?

Those aren't things that I should be thinking of. It's better to worry about the well-being of the community. There are so many things to do that I don't have time for everything. If it's not a matinée, it's the fair; if it's not the fair, it's a meeting; if it's not a meeting it's a banquet in Moisés' honor. God, the amount of money that I spend on clothes! If they only knew . . . at least Moisés' friends give me a good discount. I get so angry when I think that Kristal knows it. Her dress "with a full skirt trimmed with red lace, matching that of her fan" must have cost a fortune. Since her husband is a millionaire . . . of course she can afford luxuries like that. She can get things in the latest Paris fashion as if it were nothing. Now, I don't deny that she has taste. She was magnificent the other night. And she can sing, too.

I can't understand why Miriam kept criticizing her the whole night, and so loud that whoever was around could hear her. I even had to get up because I was so embarrassed. I told Moisés I was going to powder my nose.

But I feel sorry for Miriam, anyhow.

What am I going to wear next Sunday? Again the stole that Moisés gave me for my birthday? I guess I'm going to have to, though I'm ashamed of being seen so often in it. Maybe I'll get my black dress ready. If Jacobo dies, I'm going to have to wear it to the funeral anyway. What am I going to do? I don't own many furs. But "velvet coats are very much in fashion for afternoon wear. They have a charming line, slightly longer than last season." It's time for Moisés to buy me some new clothes. I'm the first lady of the community, and it's up to me to give the example. "In the latest fashions coat and shoes are often matching. One of the finest models, this one combines patent leather with crepe de chine."

If it weren't for me, nothing would ever get done. Things have changed from the days when that Rosenblat woman was in charge. She was full of spite, and the only reason she went to the meetings was to make trouble. Thank God she left Lima last summer. It's the first time we've been happy and in harmony for years.

What am I going to do? I still have time to go to the movies with Miriam. I'm sure she's waiting for me. Tonight I'm going to tell Moisés. It's not fair that he hasn't gone to visit his brother. He should go alone. That's it. He really should go alone.

It's not that I meddle in what is not my business, but after all, a brother is a brother, even if he is like Jacobo. What madness to have a son with an Indian woman! I really can't let him into my house. What am I going to do with a boy who isn't even one of our people? Yosef is going to have his bar-mitzvah in two years. Moisés is going to be so proud to see his son become a man! He's going to be the most beautiful little man in the whole community. We have to call the rabbi so that he can begin preparing him. I don't intend to watch pennies. Nothing is too good for my son. But what are we going to do about the bar-mitzvah of Jacobo's son? He had to be crazy to ask us to take care of it. The boy can't even go inside the synagogue. I'm sure the rabbi won't allow it. He's going to regret it, Jacobo will. He'll regret having done that dance with the Indian woman. It wasn't enough that he got involved with her, he had to give her a son, as if we didn't have Jewish women who could have given him what he was looking for. Now he wants his son to come and live with us!

Maybe Moisés is happy. Maybe that's the only way he can get Jacobo's money. And the community would speak so well of us if we take care of the child.

I'm going to ask the rabbi about it, see what he tells me to do. I'm sure he'll say the boy should stay in the village, why should we get into the mess? If he loves his son so much, why doesn't Jacobo ask him to come right now to live with him?

What can I do? The only thing I ask is that he not die today. If he does, we are going to have to cancel tomorrow's program. It's not fair to ask the children to wait now that everything is all set. Miriam is going to get so angry when she sees the changes we made in the program! Everything is going to be beautiful.

I'm going to go to Miriam's house and ask her to come with me to Jacobo's house. I can't wait to see Miriam's face when I tell her.

# Chronicles: 1930-1931

Commander Luis Sánchez Cerro stages a coup against the Government of Leguía. The revolution spreads to the capital city: the Lima Garrison demands the President's resignation, and Leguía hands over his duties to a junta headed by General Manuel Ponce.

Sánchez Cerro flies to Lima from Arequipa and assumes power. During his ride from the airport to the Presidential Palace, he is cheered by an immense crowd.

Leguía is thrown in jail with his closest aides. They will be judged by a special tribunal for the crime of having enriched themselves illicitly at the expense of the people.


Abraham Singer and Jacobo Lerner meet one evening at the Hebrew Union during a dance sponsored by the Society of Traveling Salesmen. Singer tells Jacobo he has decided to stay permanently in Lima because he has discovered his life is in danger every time he travels. When he finds out that Jacobo Lerner is still peddling in the streets of Lima, Singer proposes they open a *prostíbulo* in partnership. Thus, on the night of

February 15, five months after his return to the capital, Jacobo attends the inauguration of their house in the La Victoria quarter of the city. Afraid of incurring the wrath of the rabbi, Jacobo keeps his new business an absolute secret. Nonetheless, Singer invites some single members of the community to the inauguration.

Having miraculously survived an automobile accident, don Jacobo Lerner attends the ceremony of "Shevuoth," and promises to donate a "Sefer-Torah" for the synagogue.

In February, 1931, the military junta led by Sáchez Cerro leaves the government in the hands of Mariano Holguín, bishop of Arequipa and acting archbishop of Lima. In March, the Council of Ministers, chaired by don Elio Samanez Campo, holds national elections through secret balloting, in which Sánchez Cerro obtains a majority over his enemy, Haya de la Torre. On taking command, Sanchez Cerro declares war on all other political parties. In Miraflores, there is an attempt against his life.

A religious ceremony is held at the Jewish Cemetery of Bellavista, in which a tablet is placed on the tomb of Daniel Abramowitz, who had died on October 17, 1930. Mr. Abramowitz had been an active member of the community.

His widow donates fifty *soles* to the coffers of the Hebrew Union.

The ceremony of "Sefer-Torah" takes place amid great emotion of all the participants. The hall and the patio have been specially illuminated. When Jacobo Lerner appears with the Sefer-Torah in his arms, he is received by a large group of the most important members of the community carrying candles.

As he walks into the Hall, the orchestra starts playing the national anthem, and all present sing with enthusiasm. Next, don Jacobo hands the Sefer-Torah to Rabbi Schneider, who gives a brief speech of thanks in Hebrew.

Then Marcos Kaplan says a few words wishing for the quick recovery of the President of the Hebrew Union, don Moisés Lerner, from the illness that afflicts him.

## REPUBLIC OF PERU
District of Chepén

Bureau of Civil Registry and Statistics
BIRTHS
CERTIFICATE #274

Today, Saturday the sixth of March of nineteen hundred and thirty-one, at nine in the morning, don Samuel Edelman Rosenblat, thirty-nine years old, married, born in Vinnitsa, and domiciled at Lizardo Montero 504, Chiclayo, appeared at the town hall of this city and declared that on the fifteenth of December of nineteen hundred and twenty-five, a male child of the Caucasian race was born to don Jacobo Lerner Roseman, thirty-eight years old, white, single, born in Staraya Ushitza, a merchant by profession, and to doña Bertila Wilson Alvarado, twenty-five years old, white, born in Chepén. Said male child to be named EFRAIN.

With him, as witnesses, appeared don Manuel Polo Miranda, fifty years old, married, born in Chepén, landholder, and don León Mitrani, thirty-eight years old, single, born in Staraya Ushitza, merchant. On the declaration of whom this certificate was signed by the Mayor, the Inspector, the Section Chief, and the witnesses.

| | |
|---|---|
| Pablo Morales Santiesteban | Julio Arana Ríos |
| MAYOR | INSPECTOR |
| Antonio Paredes Sosa | Samuel Edelman Rosenblat |
| SECTION CHIEF | REGISTRANT |
| Manuel Polo Miranda | León Mitrani |
| WITNESS | WITNESS |

By order of the Mayor acting with the authority duly vested in him, this birth certificate is duly registered.

Chepén, sixth of March of nineteen hundred and thirty-one.

# XV

## *Efraín: Chepén, 1934*

GRANDFATHER BROUGHT the news home, but I already knew it. He came in like a whirlwind after I returned from the movies, screaming that old man Mitrani had died. I guess he was frightened, because he said the police were in Mitrani's house and Doctor Meneses said Mitrani had been poisoned, and they didn't know whether it was his wife who had done it, or whether the druggist had made a mistake. Zoila left immediately and said that she was going to see Manuel in the drugstore, to find out what was going on. How could they blame *him*? Everyone knew the old lady was crazy. But I didn't know why they were making so much of the business, since everyone knew Manuel makes mistakes about everything. But Grandmother said she spoke with the doctor and he said Mitrani had died of the colic and that his death was the work of the Lord.

If I say what I know they're not going to pay any attention, so I might as well keep quiet. Already they spent the day looking at me with their eyes wide open, and one day they are going to eat me alive. All that will be left of me is skin and little white bones spread throughout the house. They'll step on them, like pigs, but then, who cares?

. . . but if they are buried behind the patio, maybe a tree will grow, a green tree that will give peaches. Better not plant them where the pigs can get at them, because they would eat the tree before it had a chance to grow . .
. . . then nobody will remember, not even Aunt Francisca. She doesn't come to see me anymore, because she says Uncle Pedro is very sick and is going to die. After he is dead I don't know whether they will be able to pull his neck straight. Grandfather says you can do anything you want with dead people because they don't have any strength and they just lie there like I did that afternoon, in the church. They just lie there and they don't move or anything, but they can see everything that goes on around them, even if their eyes are closed. They can hear, if someone speaks to them, but they can't move or say anything. They say it's been months since Uncle Pedro has been out of bed, and he doesn't even get up to go to the bathroom. Aunt Francisca says he pees in the bed, and you can smell it all over the house. She says it smells like the devil.

But I no longer believe in the devil. Aunt Francisca told me all lies because she didn't want me to be like my father. Now she doesn't even come to take me to church, she just goes by herself, not like before when she came early to dress me and take me with her. I was an altar boy then. I had to help Father Chirinos say mass. He doesn't want me to help him anymore, either, and he hasn't come to see me in a long time. I don't know why. He used to love me a lot.

I bet he is embarrassed because I saw him in the main square with all those people the night they killed Mr. Mitrani. But I am not going to tell the truth to anyone for as long as I live. No one will believe me anyway. Like that time I told Grandfather I saw a dead man floating on the river, face down, slowly floating downstream through the town, and I was screaming for help but nobody came. He laughed at me, and told me he knew all my stories by heart and he wasn't going to fall for this one. But I laughed later when they found the dead man and pulled him out of the water and saw that it was Antonio, the drunk, and his face was swollen so that it looked like an old soccer ball with the leather worn by kicks.

The truth is, they are liars who are always telling me stories. Like that time they said I had gone to the river by myself and jumped into the water on the other side of the sluice, just where the water goes through, and they said I had done it on purpose. I know they were lying to me because I don't remember it at all. It was Bertila who tried to kill herself. I also don't remember going to church and kicking the Virgin Mary, which is what Father Chirinos accused me of doing. He told Aunt Francisca he found me on the altar, calling her whore because she had abandoned her son.

So they don't let me go out alone anymore. It's been a long time since I have gone to school, and Miss Angelita doesn't even ask for me. Ricardo doesn't say anything to me when he gets home from school, he hardly talks to me at all. And Aunt Francisca is always in her house, she never comes out. The lice are going to eat her up. Her face is already full of little holes, because the lice are in her body and they come out through her hair, like Grandmother, who was so full of lice that they ate her alive and she doesn't live here anymore.

Let them believe whatever they want. I'm the only one who knows the truth, and I am not going to tell anyone.

How beautiful was the movie this afternoon! But sad, too, because it made me think of my father and of Mr. Mitrani. When I told Bertila I had seen my father in church she began to laugh again and told me she was going to take me to the witch-doctor so he could get those ideas out of my head. But Aunt Francisca began to scream at her that to speak like that was a sacrilege, that she would see how I would be cured with the help of God, because he never abandoned his children.

But the night we went to the witch-doctor, the Chang woman came with us. We traveled in a truck until it was almost morning and we arrived at a spot in the desert. There were a lot of people around a bonfire with big flames, and an old man with bones in his hands was dancing around and giving such screams that I got goose bumps. Bertila said I shouldn't be afraid, he was the witch-doctor and he was going to help me. He was making something in a big cauldron and they forced me to drink it. It was so awful I vomited, but Bertila forced my mouth open and they poured it down anyway. She said it would drive all the evil spirits away. She drank some too, and later we returned to the village. I was vomiting all the way, and my whole body was shaking.

She's given up now. She doesn't even know whether I am alive or dead. Every once in a while she says there is no cure for me. Not even Doctor Meneses comes to see me anymore, because Grandfather said it was a waste of money and the best thing is for them to leave me alone, except that I shouldn't go out of the house. Iris is the only other person here. She never leaves the house, either, since what happened to her. She comes close to me and caresses my hair, and says she feels very sorry for me, and then she begins to cry. Then she goes back to bed. She tells me to keep quiet and she doesn't let me tickle her all over the place the way she used to. Not even Zoila can get her out of bed, even when she tells her that if she doesn't get up they are going to send her to the reformatory. That's why I feel sorry for Iris. She didn't do anything. Not even César could have the mayor sent to jail for what he did, and he doesn't live here anymore because he is too ashamed to stay in the village. Grandfather was right. They didn't do anything to the mayor, and Grandfather goes on selling him whatever he can. He only cares about money and really no one remembers what happened to Iris.

Grandmother used to remember, before she left. One night she loaded her cot and her trunks into a little truck and went to live with her sister in Cajamarca. She says she is never coming back because Grandfather doesn't want to sell his houses. If he dies one of these days, she says, we are all going to live in Lima.

I will see my father then. He is going to come to get me, like last time, and this time he is going to take me away from this house where no one talks to me. Not even Ricardo talks to me anymore. Zoila keeps telling him to stay away from me, that maybe whatever I have is contagious.

That's why I don't say anything anymore. When I told Aunt Francisca that I had spoken to my father in church she told me to stop making up silly tales.

Well, the curse is really going to fall on this town now. One day the water is all going to spill out above the gate and we are all going to drown. The crabs are going to eat us alive and not even Father Chirinos is going to be saved.

The movie was so sad that it made me cry. When I left the movie house I saw how a lot of people were all around Mr. Mitrani's front door, and the door was open. The mayor was with Mr. Mitrani. "Is it true that you, Mitrani, are the King of the Jews?" he asked him. But Mr. Mitrani didn't answer him. He just smiled and his eyes were very sad. Then the mayor asked all the others what they should do with someone who called himself the King of the Jews. They all answered that he should be crucified.

The mayor asked for a basin of water, and washed his hands in front of all the people. The police took Mr. Mitrani's clothes off and threw a purple cloak over him. They put a crown of thorns on his head and gave him a reed to hold in his hand. The policemen knelt in front of him and they mocked him, saluting him and calling him King of the Jews. But Mr. Mitrani smiled, and looked at them with sadness in his eyes, so that they got angry, and they began to beat him and spit at him, and finally they dragged him out into the street with his cross on his shoulders. He couldn't even walk with his lame leg, and he didn't have his cane. All the people in town were there. The mayor told the policemen to hit Mr. Mitrani with their whips until, finally they arrived at the square. They put him up on the cross and stuck a lance in his ribs and there they left him, bleeding. I don't know what else happened because I ran into the church to pray, because I knew my father would come to see me. He could only come to the church, never to the house. Nobody loves him there, not even Aunt Francisca, who goes on making the sign of the cross each time I ask her whether it is true that my father lives in Lima.

That is why I went to wait for him in the church. I was alone there because everyone else was in the square, so I began to pray very loud to see whether my father would hear me. Then I got tired and lay down on the ground. The tiles were cold like the gravestones in the cemetery, and I fell asleep. When I woke up I saw people there that I had never seen before, but I did recognize my father because he was wearing a black suit and came near me holding a bunch of red flowers in his hand.

I was stiff on the ground, and could not move. He realized I wanted to talk to him and couldn't, and he began to cry. I begged him not to cry, and Father Chirinos, too, begged him not to cry, but he went on crying because, he said, he had come from Lima to take me with him and there I was, stiff on the floor of the church like a dead man, and he could not take me.

Then they all left and once again I was alone in the church. I saw that I could move and I went running out into the street and saw the people still in the square.

My father walked by without looking at Mr. Mitrani on the cross. They just left him there, with blood dripping down his body, while everyone insulted him. If he could fly, why didn't he get off the cross? they asked him.

Suddenly the earth began to move and everything became dark and I returned home. The next morning, Mr. Mitrani's body was no longer in the square. I am sure that it went straight to heaven, he flew straight to heaven, like that Sunday he jumped from the roof of his house. I knew he flew, even though everyone in the house says he fell straight to the ground and broke all of his bones.

When I see my father I am going to tell him that Mr. Mitrani no longer lives in the village, that he flew slowly up, all the way to heaven.

# READERS' FORUM

Lima, May 13, 1933

The Editor
*Jewish Soul*

Dear Friend:

A few weeks ago we were visited at home by representatives of the Sephardic Society who were soliciting contributions toward the construction of a building for the Society.

Even though we are not Sephardic, we could not deny our help. Each made an effort according to our abilities. Some made greater sacrifices than others. We did what we could for our Sephardic brothers.

Of course, each one of us is eagerly awaiting publication by the Sephardic Society of the list of contributors, not because we want to see our own names among them, but to have the certainty that the money we have given is being used for the goal for which it was solicited.

Thanking you very much for your attention, I remain,

Sincerely yours,

MOISES LERNER

# ON THE JEWISH ORIGINS OF HITLER

According to a report published by a newspaper in Prague, and there is no reason to disbelieve it, Adolf Hitler, the blood-thirsty and picturesque dictator who controls the destiny of Germany, had a Jewish great-grandfather. Mordecai Hitler, the Führer's ancestor, renounced his religion in 1827. One century later, one of his descendants would become the greatest traitor that Israel has suffered in the long centuries of its martyrdom.

Mr. Hitler is worthy of our compassion as the shade of his ancestor comes to trouble the glory that he has so easily attained. He, who believed himself heir of Wotan, suddenly has to deal with the fact that he does not descend from a Germanic Valhalla, but rather from a miserable Austrian ghetto. Is there anything more ridiculous and more tragic than a dictator who bases his doctrine on the strength of the Germanic peoples and the extermination of the Jews? We are genuinely sorry for Mr. Adolf Hitler, Chancellor of Germany, organizer of the Third Reich, and sworn enemy of the race that has given Moses and Jesus Christ to the world. Mordecai Hitler was thrown out of the race because he was not worthy of sharing a heritage with them.

—THE EDITORS

# NEWS OF THE WORLD

## THE EFFECTS OF HITLER'S POLICIES

*Berlin*—The systematic and relentless hate campaign against German Jews has had the result that, as life in Germany becomes intolerable, more and more Jews are setting their sights on Palestine. Thus, since the new anti-Semitic campaign began, the Immigration Office is receiving countless inquiries about the possibilities of settling there.

## DANILO, A RUMANIAN ANTI-SEMITE, PREACHES LOVE TOWARD THE JEWS

*Bucharest*—H. Danilo, leader of the anti-Semitic organization "Iron Guard," has surprised everyone with his declaration recanting his previous opinions and exhorting all Christians to love the Jews. In several meetings that have taken place recently, he has expressed the idea that anti-Semitism poisons rural youth and students alike, and is extremely damaging to the whole population.

"The whole country," he said, "including our Jewish brothers, thinks I organized the Borscha pogrom. That is not true. Neither I, nor my colleague Berindli, have ever been anti-Semites, and I hope we will never become so in the future."

Jewish sources in Besarabia suspect that Danilo's attitude is the fruit of political calculations. Since he has become associated with the Nationalist Party, it is believed that he is trying by these means to assure himself of the Jewish vote in the coming elections.

# Chronicles: 1932-1933

On the morning of September 1st, Alférez Díaz, carrying two pieces of light artillery, takes up a position on an island approximately 1500 yards away from the town of Leticia, on the Amazon River. Alférez La Rosa, with the remaining troops and with a heavy machine gun, lands at Leticia. After firing a few rounds, the machine gun jams, and he gives orders for the fusiliers to advance.

The Colombians return fire sporadically, until Mayor Villamil, concluding that further resistance would be to no avail, flies a white flag on the balcony of his residence.

Afterward, the flag of Peru is flown from City Hall, a coded message is sent by radio to Iquitos notifying the command post that Leticia has been taken, and the inhabitants of that city are told one more time that their home is part of the national territory.

On a warm spring Sunday, at about the time when the church bells ring calling everyone to mass, Samuel Edelman appears in Chepén with a small leather suitcase and a thick pile of magazines. When he gets off the bus he walks directly to the house of León Mitrani. Mitrani is in his shirtsleeves and he is wearing his philacteries. A thin leather thong snakes up his left arm, and between forefinger and thumb he holds a small cube of wood sheathed in leather inside which there is a piece of parchment inscribed with sections of the Bible. Another thong surrounds his forehead, at the end of which is a second cube of identical dimensions, material, and contents as the first. He is wearing a black and white shawl over his head and partially over his shoulders. It is decorated with bold Hebrew letters.

Ill-humored because he has been interrupted in his morning prayers, Mitrani beckons Edelman in with a harsh gesture. The room is dark except where the sun shows in yellow lines through the slits of the shuttered window. Wasting no time, Edelman tells Mitrani he has brought him several issues of *Jewish Soul* magazine. Edelman leaves his suitcase on the table, picks up one of the magazines, walks with it toward the light, silently reads a few paragraphs to refresh his memory, and then tells Mitrani what has brought him there: the situation of the Jews in Germany is disastrous; thousands have been driven from their homes, stripped of all their belongings, and, in general, mistreated physically and spiritually. The situation worsens day by day. Jewish lawyers and doctors have been forbidden to practice their professions. The Nazis swarm the streets shouting "Juden, werrecke!" and whenever they meet a Jew, they strip him naked and beat him.

Before Edelman has finished speaking, Mitrani jumps to his feet and solemnly exclaims: "My prophecies have begun to come true! Soon the Germans will come to Chepén!"


In 1933, the former President of the Junta, Commander Jiménez, dies during an aborted revolution.


On the 30th of April, President Luis Sánchez Cerro inspects the troops at the race track in Santa Beatriz. Afterward, as he returns in an open car, a terrorist shoots him with a pistol fired at close range. Fatally wounded, he is taken to the Italian Hospital, where he dies a short time later.

Six months after his first visit, Samuel Edelman shows up in Chepén on a Saturday morning and stays with León Mitrani. Toward noon, while Mitrani is absorbed in his habitual prayers, the sounds of a band begin. Mitrani interrupts his prayers and runs to the street, followed closely by Edelman. There, they see a detachment of soldiers marching behind a military band. Mitrani begins screaming: "The Germans! The Germans are here!" He runs back into the house and hides in the attic. Edelman tries to make him leave his hiding place, but he cannot convince Mitrani that the soldiers are Peruvian and that they are only marching through the town on their way north.

On May 26 troops from Colombia attack the garrison at Gueppi, on the Peruvian side of the river. As wave after wave of airplanes hit their positions, the Peruvians retreat. Only a single officer, Lieutenant Teodoro Garrido Leca, holds out until his last machine gun is silenced. Peruvian dead: 15. Peruvian wounded and prisoners: 30. Colombian dead: 5. Colombian wounded: 10.

Congress names General Oscar R. Benavidez President of the Republic.

The Jewish community decides to donate an ambulance to the Peruvian Red Cross. During the ceremonies, Mr. Moisés

Lerner, President of the Hebrew Union, makes the following speech:

Mr. President of the Peruvian Red Cross, Ladies and Gentlemen:

Because of this ceremony, this day is a memorable one for us, the community of Jews living in Peru, the country we consider our homeland.

In the name of the Jewish community I have the pleasure of giving the keys to this ambulance to the Committee that is here to receive them, satisfied because we have contributed in a small way to the humanitarian task of the Peruvian Red Cross in the creation of a greater Peru.

This is the beloved homeland to which every Jew living here feels heartfelt allegiance.

Long live Peru, ladies and gentlemen!

Long live the President!

Long live the Peruvian Red Cross!

# XVI

## *Juana Paredes: Lima, December 21, 1935*

I FEEL like staying in bed for the rest of the day, I had such a horrible dream, but if I don't hurry up I'm going to miss the mass at nine. Confession afterward, and is it going to be cold in church at this hour. The best thing is not to look Padre Dávalos in the face . . .

Cold, graveyard cold, like in the dream, cold as those white marble niches that stiffen the bones. It sneaks through the cracks in the confession box, the cold.

Bah, the pills the druggist gave me are good for nothing! I must be getting old. The first signal of old age is tiredness. That's what he told me last night, the druggist. The trouble is, I haven't slept well for weeks. I think, think all night, until my head feels as if it is about to explode. And when I sleep? I have dreams like that one last night. That's as good as not sleeping at all.

I'm going to tell that druggist. I want my money back. I need every penny, what with seven boys whatever Jacobo gives me never lasts to the end of the month. Marcos left Delia nothing but debts. We've even had to sell the sewing machine and now we go around dressed like beggars. Before, at least I made my own dresses. I never asked Jacobo to buy anything at all for me. And we constantly have to buy on credit at the store on the corner so that I don't want to go anymore because I'm so ashamed. It's better that my sister goes and fights for a little food. After all, they are her children.

What's going to happen when he dies? I already told Delia that no matter what, we would manage, that we are not going to beg from those Jews. They owe us nothing and we owe them nothing. Anyway, I don't think Jacobo is going to be so mean as not to leave us anything. Or we'll be in the street, because who remembers us?

I would be happy with little. With a little money every month so that we can live, I would be satisfied. It would be nothing for him. He's not going to take his furniture and his silver where he is going.

I was the one who helped him furnish the house. That house, always so cold. It was a woman that it needed.

He is not going to be able to abandon the children of Marcos, even though he says they're not Jewish. And me? I gave up the best years of my life at his side. And I'm sure he'll remember me in his will.

I'm not going to see him now because he closed the door in my face. I don't want him to believe that I have no self-respect and that I am only interested in his money.

But who is he going to leave it to?

I never asked him for money, even though I more than deserved it. Delia says I shouldn't be an idiot and I should ask him for what is mine by rights. So I told her she had nothing to worry about, Jacobo has a heart of gold. When Marcos died he didn't have to give us anything if he did not want to. He did it because he was good and compassionate and because he promised.

Delia will be coming home from church soon and she is going to begin with the same song again. It would be much better if she minded her own business, because I haven't asked her for her advice. If I get dressed quickly I can get out of the house before she returns and that way I'll be left in peace until afternoon.

Afternoon! That's when the whole family gets together to ask me where the money that Jacobo gave me is. The truth is I can't stand these Sundays since Jacobo fell sick. It's not the same as it used to be. I used to go to his house in the morning and spend the whole day listening to the record player. I was served like a queen. The maid had to call me "Madame" and used to die from envy.

I would have taken care of everything if he had let me, and then he wouldn't have had to pay that worthless old woman a penny. Now when he dies she is going to steal everything and nobody will be there to see that she doesn't.

God knows what Jacobo has in his head. What would Marcos have said? What is Delia going to say? Once, Padre Dávalos went to their house to demand that Marcos marry Delia, but Marcos threw him out. Delia was fine for the bedroom, he said, but not fine enough to become his wife according to law.

And as if Delia herself had cared one way or the other. Not two weeks after I met Jacobo she used to arrange to leave us alone in the house. She, Marcos, and the children would all take his taxi somewhere and not return until late at night. Then she used to smile at me like an accomplice who understands everything. Jacobo used to get red as a beet from embarrassment, but the truth is, she understood nothing, because Jacobo always behaved toward me like a perfect gentleman. He treated me like a lady. He never as much as touched me in that house. Not that I would have allowed him to, because I have my self-respect, and he would have thought that I was that way with everyone.

He was shy. I don't know what he was afraid of, but he was shy. I had to take the initiative, because otherwise we would still be sitting like dolls in that parlor. And when we began seeing each other in his house, if I hadn't started I would never have felt his hand anywhere on my body.

And then Delia asking when we were going to get married, whether I was happy with the relationship as it was, and all kinds of things. Sure I was happy. Of course, if he had asked me to marry him I wouldn't have said no. I'm not stupid. But I never had any illusions about becoming his wife. There, God is my witness.

It's too late to start thinking about those things now. Now the best thing is to go to church and to go to confession. It's been a long time. What is Padre Dávalos going to say? "Let us, with Jesus, walk toward death without fear, because death is not the end of everything. Death is our destiny, but to die with Jesus, and like Jesus, for others, is to live the life that has no end. . . ." But Jacobo's life ends now, and the truth is, I should have followed the Padre's advice.

But what does Padre Dávalos know about what I feel for Jacobo? I wasn't going to go and listen to him speak against the Jews. He hates the Jews because Marcos paid no attention whatever to him. When Marcos died Padre Dávalos almost did not want to bury him and he told Delia that at last she would be free from sin.

So he is going to say the same thing to me. He is going to be very happy that Jacobo is dying. I'm not going to give him that pleasure. I'd rather stay in bed all morning long. Jacobo is probably already dead, and I don't know one way or the other. What a horrible dream I had last night! I saw Jacobo on a narrow road, I saw him climb rock after rock toward an abyss, I saw him throw himself down, but before he reached the bottom he vanished in the air. Then I saw him again surrounded by trees without leaves. And then again, suddenly, the landscape changed, and he was at the bottom of the sea, and a red sun was descending on his head. His face was as pale as a dead man's. He looked at me from under the water, and his look was cold but also affectionate, sad but also happy. He began to make gestures, calling to me, and I started to walk away, backward, farther and farther, until I didn't see him any more, until I reached a hallway full of niches, and in one of them, without a casket, was Jacobo's naked body.

Delia is going to tell me that is a sure signal Jacobo is already dead.

Well, if he doesn't want to see me, that's his business. God knows I never meddled in his affairs. I didn't even say anything about the whorehouse. I didn't even care about that. I told Delia it was better than being a taxi driver. I don't complain, and I don't regret. I did everything I did with my eyes wide open, and I have never been ashamed of it.

Let my sister come and say something to me. Not only does she have no right, but my situation is a hundred times better than hers. What did she get from living with Marcos Geller? With her luck she found the only poor Jew in Lima. The only thing he did was fill her up with children and leave her in misery. Other Jews were getting rich like nothing, and poor Marcos was still driving his taxi.

With little better luck, how different my life with Jacobo would have been! I'm sure that when he saw Marcos so poor and so sick, with his children who weren't even Jews, Jacobo got frightened. That was his problem. He was always frightened of everything. He was frightened of life. You really had to see him on the day that Marcos died! He screamed at Delia that he should be given a Jewish burial, and I practically had to drag him to the funeral. But when he saw that my sister wasn't about to change her mind for anything in the world, he paid all the expenses because what mattered was to get him buried, and he had no alternative.

But he demanded that Marcos' body be put in a niche. He said some strange thing about dead people not wanting to be inside the ground, and that he would be safer in a niche. Then I remembered what had happened to a friend of his in the village where his son lives; he told me no one knew where the body was, and surely it must be wandering on the highways without rest.

None of Marcos' friends came to the funeral. Jacobo was the only one, and he spent the whole time with his head bent, as if he were crying. I have to admit he is the most tender man I've ever seen. He was the only one who helped us later. He didn't have to do it.

But now if I go to confession, Padre Dávalos is going to speak against him and scold me because I have been living in sin all this time. What does he know about these things?

Father, I confess before Almighty God that I have sinned in word and deed . . . what? That I didn't want to be a spinster for the rest of my life?

I never told him. It would have been a waste of time.

Every day Delia was on my back. At least ask him to set you up in a house, she used to say. But how could I do something so low? He never promised me anything. He didn't say, if you do this I'll do that.

I never meddled in his affairs, that has to be said. And I obeyed him in everything. Sometimes, in my dreams, I saw myself as his wife, surrounded by our children, going out to elegant places, dressed in luxurious clothes, like a lady, but . . .

Of course what Delia wanted was to get rid of me. The idiot didn't realize that if Jacobo gave her money it was because I was living here. We never lacked for anything. No luxuries, that's true. I never asked him for luxuries, nor would I have accepted them. That would have been selling my body.

What am I going to confess if I go? That I have sinned, period? Where have I sinned, Father? For the last four years I have been going to bed with an infidel. He is an infidel but he is good, Father. He is a fine man, Father. He is charitable. Mortal sin? God has punished him and he is going to die, Father? I beg you to take pity on him, Father. Can you give absolution to an infidel? The sins of the flesh are the worst sins, Father? You can't do anything for him, Father? And me, Father, can you give me absolution? In what have I sinned, Father? I allowed Jacobo to take advantage of me? He didn't want to marry me because I am not Jewish? I understand, Father, I had no claims. He did with me what he wanted, and when he didn't want to see me, he shut the door in my face. Like when they took him to that hospital. I never even found out what he had. I'm sure his brother had him shut up in there so that he could steal his money again.

It was months of not knowing and of waiting. I even thought I would never see him again, because of all that time without news. And then he came back home as if nothing had happened and I like a fool was happy that he was there, and we started seeing each other again. I didn't ask him why he had done or why he had not done. I didn't care. It was better than being alone in my sister's house again.

Jacobo never even understood that was my only motive. From the beginning he told me again and again not to have any illusions, that he would never marry me, that he would never marry. But he did want to get married to his sister-in-law's sister. I never reproached him for that. Do whatever you want, I told him. Now I don't even know whether Delia was right or not in going to see her. She pretended she was me, and told her I don't know what stories about what we did. She said she did it because of me, because it wasn't right. If he wanted to get married, there I was, to give him children and take care of his house.

Then the wedding was canceled, and things worked out this way. If he had married he wouldn't be dying alone now. And what makes me angrier is that I would have been so happy to take care of him and his house without getting married or anything. I never said I wanted to be his wife. I would have given him a son that was like him in everything. He wouldn't be dying alone now. He doesn't even know his own son! Now he wants to bring him here and give him to his sister-in-law. I told him I would take care of him as if he were my own!

He laughed. He laughed like a madman. Told me that his son was Jewish, and he would not allow him to be brought up in a Christian house.

But I would take care of him. Not for the money. No, not for the money, but to keep some remembrance of Jacobo. I'm sure his son will grow up to be like him and he will be a good man in everything.

His whole family has abandoned him and now the poor man is going to die completely alone and we are going to have to bury him in a niche, next to Marcos. I'm going to pray loud so they can all hear me and take pity on his poor soul.

Oh, all-merciful God, listen to my prayer for the soul of Jacobo, your servant whom you called today from this world. Do not abandon him in the hands of our enemy, but take him in yours to heaven with your holy angels, because he always believed in you. Spare him from the pains of hell and give him the eternal happiness of your kingdom. Amen.

If he only let me in to see him one last time. He would believe that I only came to ask for something, but anyway, I'm going to pray an Our Father for him. He'll straighten things out with his god when the moment comes. He must be very afraid of God, because one day he told me that his god was cruel and vengeful, not like Jesus Christ, who takes pity on his children.

I wonder where souls go, after death? I'm going to ask Padre Dávalos if Jews and Christians are in the same heaven. I'd better go to church before Delia comes home with the children . . . but, what am I going to confess to, if I go?

# Chronicles: 1934

An aerial combat takes place on the 14th of February. Three Peruvian seaplanes attack a Colombian expeditionary force going up river toward Tarapacá, and shortly after, three Colombian aircraft appear, engaging them in a dog fight. Two of the Peruvian planes are forced to flee. The third, piloted by Alférez Secada, continues to fight. Secada distinguishes himself by the control he has over his craft. He turns off the engine, simulating that he has been hit, and then, at less than one hundred meters altitude, he releases his last bomb. It strikes the stern of the "Córdoba," but does not detonate. Secada flees in the direction of Leticia, with the Colombian planes in close pursuit.

In a deserted area of the road between Chepén and Chimbote, the casket containing the body of León Mitrani is lost in a sand storm.

On the 15th of February, at 7:30 in the morning, cruisers on the river begin an artillery attack on the hill of Tarapacá. At

8:00, planes strafe the area. After another hour of continuous bombardment, the Colombian troops disembark. They capture a Krupp cannon, manufactured in 1894, five Mauser carbines, one Hotchkiss #13 submachine gun, and twelve cases of ammunition. At 9:00 the Colombian flag waves over the summit of Tarapacá.

On June 19 the Commission from the League of Nations hands over the Amazon Territory to Colombian authorities.

After a long and painful illness, don Marcos Geller, 37 years old, dies in Callao. He leaves behind a wife and children. In spite of the many protests of Rabbi Theodore Schneider, Geller's widow decides that the remains of her husband are to be deposited at the Cemetery of the Angels, where they will receive Christian burial.

# INAUGURATION OF THE NEW BUILDING OF THE HEBREW UNION

On the night of the inauguration, everyone present expressed great satisfaction with the new building. Happiness and contentment marked each and every face, and everyone was pleased to have, at long last, such a luxurious meeting place decorated with so much good taste. Our President, don Moisés Lerner, opening the premises, read the following speech that was vigorously applauded:

Dear Ladies and Fellow Members of the Club:

In our meeting tonight we are celebrating the success of our efforts in saving this, our first institution. I do not exaggerate if I tell you that it almost disappeared for good, but I, as a President conscious of his responsibilities, could not tolerate the loss of something that our community so sorely needs.

I would like to give you some of its history. About a month and a half ago, don Jacobo Fishman came to my store and told me that we could no longer buy the house on Zavala Street, where our club used to be located, and that it was scheduled for demolition. The next day I called an extraordinary meeting: eighteen members attended. Eighteen, ladies and gentlemen, is the number that in Hebrew signifies life. I explained to them the grave danger faced by our Society. We decided to form a committee to take charge of the reorganization of our Society, and here you have what the committee has achieved since it began its work forty days ago.

Forty days was the period of time Moses took to bring us the Ten Commandments. The law will exist as long as there are men. I will be satisfied if our Society lasts a little less than that. . . .

This elegant and spacious building has everything we need. There is a room for the Yiddish school, most fundamental for me; there is a hall for programs and parties, and there is a library for the members.

You know all the efforts that have gone toward making this building a reality. I hope you will be good members and take an active part in governing the Society. It is a sublime sacrifice to work for our fellow man, especially in the case of a community such as this one.

Gentlemen: let us thank Peru, the hospitable country that protects us under its flag.

Long live Peru!

Long live the Hebrew Union!

# NEWS FROM AROUND THE WORLD

## JEWS MURDERED ON THE BORDER OF RUSSIA AND RUMANIA

*Bucharest*—Six young Jewish people of both sexes, between the ages of sixteen and twenty, were shot at this border when they attempted to cross it. Jewish deputies have protested to the Minister of War because in his declarations he said the young people in question were Communists.

*Bucharest*—A state of siege has been declared in the town of Soroke because of the presence of ten thousand Jews at the burial of the six young people murdered by the border police. The rabbi asked for the authorities' assurance that order would be maintained. His request went unheeded. As the procession went by, all Jewish-owned stores were closed as a sign of mourning.

*Vienna*—Max Reinhardt, the famous man of the theater, has declared the following in his visit to this city: "My real name is Goldman. I was born in a small village of Slovakia. I never hide either my religion or my origin. I consider myself a practicing Jew, and I am not ashamed to say that this year, as in all previous years, I fasted on Yom Kippur. I believe in my heart and in my soul. When on the eve of Rosh Hashana I visit my parents' grave, I feel doubly Jewish."

# MEDICAL COLUMN

We will concern ourselves in this article with the inherited predisposition of Jews toward a psychopathology that is more moral than intellectual. We might say that this neurosis is the one produced by moral pain exacerbated by excessive intellectual work. This state has the following symptoms: Headaches, insomnia, palpitations, cold sweats, gastro-intestinal disturbances, and acute depression.

Anxiety is what most torments these neurotics. They have phobias. They feel incapable of facing life. They become isolated from the world around them. The etiology of neurosis among Jews is the following one:

(a) Genetic predisposition
(b) Severe moral upheavals
(c) Problems of a sexual nature
(d) Intellectual fatigue

Of all of these, the first cause is by far the most essential one. Apparently, neurotics do not love anyone. For them, it would be better to be dead, though they seldom have enough courage to commit suicide.

DR. BERNARDO RABINOWITZ

# XVII

TOWARD THE middle of 1934, Jacobo Lerner began to feel that
he had been possessed by the spirit of León Mitrani, that
Mitrani had taken refuge within him and was nourishing himself with his blood. From that moment on, his life, until then
discrete, defined by a walk in the evening through the Parque
de la Reserva or by an afternoon of love with doña Juana, began
to be disturbed by strange events, until the compact order of
his days tumbled like a castle made of sand.

Since 1929, when after his second return to Lima he
decided to open the *prostíbulo* of La Victoria, Jacobo had
shown up at the Synagogue of Breña on several occasions. The
last time had been when he handed the "Sefer-Torah" to Rabbi
Schneider. After that, he never returned, and was completely
cut off from his religion. By his own will he had been expelled
from the ancestral matrix, had cut the umbilical cord that tied
him to the universe. Not even in the nervous solitude of his
own home did he fulfill his obligations as a Jew, which he had
once considered the only source of order in his chaotic life.

During those five years he seldom visited his brother
Moisés. Each time he did his visit had an almost religious
nature; his return home was too suffocating. He preferred to
spend his leisure time at the house of Marcos Geller, who was
married to Juana Paredes' sister. In Marcos' company, Jacobo
felt freer, distant from the life that he had planned for himself
and that now belonged to Moisés. To visit Marcos Geller meant
returning unharmed, with his feet firmly planted on the

cobblestones of the street, while leaving his brother's house made him feel a musty figure, hesitating at every step, his soul full of old shipwrecks.

With doña Juana, it was as if he were in a familiar landscape, on a wide plain that reminded him of Bertila's diffused shyness. With Juana he didn't feel the anxiety that he felt with Sara, nor the deep loneliness of dirty pillows and rented rooms.

After Marcos Geller died, Jacobo cultivated the friendship of other Jews who, like him, had no family. Men deformed by solitude, whose dreams were shaped by illusions. They met, usually, at Jacobo's whorehouse, where they would give themselves heart and soul to the dissonant atmosphere. On these nights their lust went unbounded, and they left the marks of their emptiness on the bodies of the courtesans.

It was during this period that Jacobo Lerner began to feel that he was possessed by a *dybbuk,* specifically the wandering soul of León Mitrani.

The first consequence of this belief was that he left Abraham Singer in charge of the brothel and locked himself in his house, where he spent all his time studying the Bible and the Talmud. Or he floated through the rooms of his house listening at the walls, peering into the darkness of each corner.

As time went on, the emptiness of his past life began to fill with something he scarcely understood, but to which he gave himself without hesitation. It was like diving into a well of warm, comforting waters. Moved by his fervor, Jacobo began to go to the synagogue every day for both morning and afternoon prayers. With his shawl on his shoulders, he would walk from his house to the temple, arousing first astonishment and then mockery from the people in the neighborhood. He seemed not to notice those who stopped in the street to look at him, nor those who made jokes at his expense. He walked slowly, holding a corner of the *talis* in each hand, his head high, his mind full of images of Chepén as he relived, step by step, the route from Mitrani's house to his store. When the ash-colored synagogue came into his view he breathed deeply and hurried his step. The synagogue became the new vessel for all of Jacobo Lerner's emotions. There, protected from the disquieting murmurs that issued from the walls of his house, he found he could give himself wholly to God.

During one of the religious holidays, incited by a mysterious force that he could not resist, Jacobo went to the synagogue to reprimand the congregation for their sinful lives. For weeks he had been terrified by images of total destruction; his head was full of horrendous scenes in which the Jewish community of Lima perished in enormous columns of fire.

It was the second day of Shevuoth when Jacobo Lerner rushed into the temple and began shouting verses from the Prophets in his strong, powerful voice. The rabbi, who was praying in front of the tabernacle, stopped and tried to talk to him above the din of his imprecations and above the laughter and voices of the others telling Jacobo to shut up and go home.

Finally, the rabbi was able to convince him to leave, but Jacobo did not go home. Instead he sat outside the door of the temple, exhausted and thoughtful. When, some time later, people began to leave, Jacobo resumed his diatribe. His voice breaking with anger, he asked them to notice the luxury of their dress; he reproached them for their devotion to everything material; he dared them to think of the way they had abandoned everything spiritual. When the rabbi saw Jacobo in the middle of the street wielding his index finger as if it were a threatening whip of fire, prophesying the Last Judgment, he thought he understood, with a fleeting shudder, just what was wrong with him. Calmly he walked toward Jacobo, and with a loving tone in his voice, offered him his help.

But Jacobo insisted he could not be helped by a false representative of God.

One week after this incident, his brother Moisés took him to see Doctor Bernardo Rabinowitz. When, after long and careful observation, the doctor concluded that Jacobo should be hospitalized so that he might get the rest he needed, and avoid the possibility of harming himself, Moisés Lerner congratulated himself on his good luck. Thus, on the afternoon of June 2, 1934, Jacobo Lerner was admitted to the hospital at Orrantia del Mar.

# MEMBERS OF THE COMMUNITY

## MOISES LERNER

Don Moisés Lerner is one of the most important leaders in our community, and as such, his assistance will be absolutely necessary to anyone trying to reorganize our institutions.

In the early days of his presidency, some sectors of the community mistrusted him, thinking he had been elected solely because of his solid financial position. Behind the scenes, they expressed reservations about his deeds and his statements. Nonetheless, another group backed him in everything he did, because many people recognized in Mr. Lerner a seriousness and an immense capacity for work. It didn't take long before the second group included everyone in the community. Through his own merits, don Moisés Lerner has earned the love and respect of all who came in contact with him.

Lerner is a "self-made" man. At a very early age, well before his schooling was finished, he was wrenched from his home in Russia. In the hard battle that we all know, he spent some time in Germany, and finally came to Peru, where he worked, fought, and worked, and thanks to his honesty and determination built up an enviable business. Here he made his home, in a country that he deeply loves.

Don Moisés Lerner is an exemplary father and husband, a loyal friend, and above all, a good man, always willing to help his neighbor, without regard to race or nationality.

—THE EDITORS

# MEDICAL COLUMN

## OUR READERS ASK

QUESTION:

On his doctor's advice a relative of mine has been living in Jauja for the past two years since he has a lung disease. Do you think, Doctor, that after this time, we could bring him back to Lima? Or do you think it is possible that here he would suffer a relapse?

ABRAHAM METZ

ANSWER:

Although the climate of Lima is not the best for those with diseases of the lungs, if X-rays and sputum analyses indicate that he is better, he could be moved to a resort area such as Magdalena or San Miguel, of course under medical supervision.

QUESTION:

Thanking you in advance for the answer that I know you will give my question, I am addressing you because of the following problem. For the last several days I have had to stay in bed with severe back pains and inflamed kidneys. Lately, I have also been having pains in the stomach, and suffer from constipation that has become almost chronic. I habitually have to resort to laxatives and purges to relieve this complaint. What must I do to suffer less?

JACOBO LERNER

ANSWER:

Unless other symptoms, or a urine analysis, demonstrate specifically that there is something wrong with the kidneys, they are not always the cause of back pains. As far as being constipated, I advise you to eat less meat, eggs, and chocolate, and to eat more fruit, green vegetables, and black bread.

If it is only a case of improper diet, your constipation will immediately get better. If it does not, you will require a complete examination.

QUESTION:

I think I have stomach ulcers, since always I have heartburn and nausea after meals. Am I right in thinking I have ulcers?

JORGE SHULMAN

ANSWER:

The vagueness of your symptoms makes it impossible for me to give you a certain answer. Only after a thorough examination could I give you a definite diagnosis.

---

## DR. BERNARDO RABINOWITZ

PHYSICIAN-SURGEON

Specialist in diseases of the lungs, heart, and stomach

Office Hours: 10 AM to 5 PM
354 Valladolid Street

Phone: 36200

---

# HEROIC CHARACTER OF THE JEWISH SPIRIT

(Exclusive for *Jewish Soul)*

Each race has achieved, within the confines of history, its own definition of the human spirit. Notwithstanding the fact that humanity is all one, Jews have always been distinguished by adherence to their traditional morality, by their admirable sense of faith, and by the heroic nature of their lives.

Because they have the faculty of total resignation, Jews have been able to survive as a nation with no territory without losing their strong, vital traditions. More than once they have proven that the strength of an ideal is far stronger than any threat or any physical punishment. Through the ages they have divided their energies between their homes and families on the one hand, and the work of the mind on the other. Einstein, Freud, Bergson, etc., are a few examples of those Jews who have made intellectual contributions in fields ranging from the aesthetic to the scientific.

DR. MANUEL PAZ SOLDAN

# XVIII

THE ONLY person who visited Jacobo Lerner while he was at Orrantia del Mar Hospital was his sister-in-law. Moved by his misfortune, she had promised herself not to abandon him to his luck. She did not know she had assumed a responsibility she didn't really want, one that filled her with anxiety each time she went to the hospital, against her husband's wishes. She would arrive with a bunch of flowers, assuming an air of optimism to crush the disgust that Jacobo's wasted appearance produced within her. From the beginning, her visits were absurd little dramas played to the same conclusion. Shaken by the depths to which Jacobo had descended, she decided to resist all possibilities of getting close to him.

Once she found him resting in the shade of a fig tree. He was leaning against the trunk, his legs bent against his chest, his hands weakly clasping his knees, his head sunk, and his eyes fixed on nothing. He had been in that position for hours, imagining he was in León Mitrani's orchard, surrounded by dry, spiny bushes, ignoring the blind woman. Sara sat down next to him. Vaguely perceiving his sister-in-law's presence, Jacobo remained motionless and said nothing. He continued thinking of Chepén, trying to look through the thick fog. Nevertheless, all the muscles in his body tightened in response to the woman sitting next to him.

She began to talk mechanically about the day before when there had been a dinner in honor of Moisés. She described in detail the atmosphere of the Hebrew Union and gave the name of every guest. Carried on by the flow of her own words, she commented on the dresses worn by the women, admiring the taste of some, and sarcastically reproving that of others. Tenderly, she spoke of how proud and content Moisés had been, seeing the affection that was felt for him by the community.

With each passing second Jacobo went deeper into regions peopled by barely recognizable silhouettes. Indefinite streets and houses waved in his mind as he relived events from his past. Sometimes he saw himself with a cane in his hand, walking down the streets of Chepén. Other times he was praying in a room with shuttered windows, or preaching in the square in front of the church. He was publicly reproved by the priest. Guards took him from his house and dragged him through the streets. He was almost murdered by the people of Chepén. They dragged him to the square in the middle of the village. He had a cloak over his shoulders, and thin drops of blood were flowing down his forehead, clouding his eyes. Above the sea of ashen faces he saw the shape of a cross raised in the middle of the square. He broke away and began to run toward the outskirts of the village, followed by guards with whips and clubs.

On his first night in the hospital, Jacobo had had this same vision. Roused by his screams, two nuns had come into his room and found him crouching on the ground, his eyes tightly shut, shaking with fear. One of them had stayed by his side the rest of the night. The next morning, Jacobo asked her to remove the plaster crucifix from his room.

Jacobo's condition continued to deteriorate. He began to argue with the nuns about certain passages in the Bible. With vehement tone, he maintained that nowhere in the New Testament are the Jews blamed for the crucifixion of Christ. Each time he started on one of his speeches, the nuns listened to him with feigned attention, shaking their heads in compassionate agreement, not needing to contradict his words. But when Jacobo began to talk to them in Yiddish, the nuns stared at him, confused and frightened, because they believed they were in the presence of someone for whom there was no help.

After three months Jacobo had not improved, so Doctor Rabinowitz decided to release him. Convinced there was nothing more that medical science could do, he asked Rabbi Schneider to help his patient. Thus, on the 3rd of August, 1934, Jacobo left the hospital still believing the spirit of León Mitrani inhabited his body. Accompanied by Doctor Rabinowitz, he went to the house of Rabbi Schneider, who had promised to exorcise Mitrani's spirit and force him to find another dwelling place.

The rabbi, who lived about four blocks away from the synagogue, received Jacobo with great warmth and offered Jacobo lodging in his house until the exorcism began to take effect. It would be a difficult task. While the maid prepared a room, he told Jacobo with excitement that it had been a long time since he had had a chance to deal with a *dybbuk*. The last time had been in Poland, in 1915, when he practiced an exorcism on a young girl who thought herself possessed by the spirit of a whore.

The room they prepared for Jacobo was on the second floor. The furniture was scant and modest: under the window there was an old wooden bed, and next to it, on the wall, a shelf with a copper candelabra whose candles gave out a weak but turbulent light and leaden smoke. Jacobo saw only the maid, who came up three times a day to bring him his meals, and the rabbi, who came up every night in his black cloak and bonnet. He would ask Jacobo to undress and stand in the middle of the room, then walk around him, reciting obscure cabalistic formulas.

On the third night, Jacobo began to feel a change. Mitrani's spirit suddenly became imperious. Jacobo's condition worsened: for seven days and seven nights his body was racked by tremors; he saw strange images in front of his eyes; he thought the maid was a blind woman who came to give him evil potions; he mistook the rabbi for the priest of Chepén. Jacobo began to pray to God to come to his rescue.

One night Jacobo Lerner saw himself surrounded by insects that came in under the door, and he became convinced that God would never again listen to him. To escape from his prison he opened the window, went out on the ledge, opened his arms wide, and flexed his knees in order to jump. But Rabbi

Schneider, who had chanced to come in, grabbed him by his shirttails and stopped him from jumping. It was then that Jacobo realized God had in fact listened to his prayers, and had sent an angel to stop him from fleeing so that he might become completely exorcised.

Jacobo slowly began to regain his sense of reality. Recognizable faces and places once again filled his memory, and his imagination brought up images that were familiar and well defined. He saw his parents' house. He remembered a crossing on a ship. Bertila, the son he did not know, Juana Paredes and Sara Lerner, his brother Moisés, Daniel Abramowitz who had committed suicide, Marcos Geller, buried in the Cemetery of the Angels, his whorehouse, all came to mind.

But although he was regaining his sanity, he was sunk into a deeper depression than ever, because all these images were of a reality that he did not want to confront.

On the night of the 17th of August, Rabbi Schneider finally succeeded, and the spirit of León Mitrani abandoned Jacobo's body through the big toe of his right foot. With a restless flame in his eyes, the rabbi invoked Mitrani by his Hebrew name, and asked him to depart from Jacobo's body. There was a strangely familiar tone in the rabbi's invocation, as if he himself had known León Mitrani in the old days. Then Jacobo remembered what Mitrani had told him one afternoon in Chepén: a rabbi had come to the village on a donkey and stayed at his house for a few days. He had taught him some cabalistic formulas that enabled him to fly. What Jacobo had then thought to be the product of a diseased mind now had a meaning of its own, and reentered his mind as a real fact. When the exorcism was over, Jacobo noticed that blood was flowing from a small opening in his toe.

The next morning as Jacobo was getting ready to leave the rabbi's house, the rabbi told him, in an admonishing voice, that *dybbuks* pursued those who kept a secret sin, and that if he had been possessed by a wandering soul, it was to atone for his guilt.

# ON JEWS IN PERU

(Exclusive for *Jewish Soul*)

## FRAY GREGORIO GARCIA AND HIS THESIS ABOUT THE JEWS AS POSSIBLE COLONIZERS OF AMERICA

In his work entitled *The Origins of the Indians,* Fray Gregorio García holds the theory that there might have been a Jewish migration to America. He discusses in some detail the possible routes by which the lost tribes of Israel could have arrived from Greenland, to Mexico, and then Central and South America.

## INTERESTING COMPARISONS BETWEEN JEWS AND INDIANS THAT ARE ESTABLISHED IN THE BOOK:

(1) The lack of receptivity the Indians demonstrated toward the teachings of missionaries is seen as a result of atavisms of Jewish teachings.

(2) The great similarity in the footwear and clothes is remarked upon: sandals and tunics.

(3) The use of certain religious ornaments by the Indians is seen as identical to their use in Mosaic Law.

(4) Indian facial features are such that Gomara wrote, "When the conquistadores arrived with Pizarro they found Indians with Judaic faces."

(5) The custom among Indians of raising their arms to the heavens to give emphasis to what they are saying is seen to be much like a gesture of the prophets of Israel. The messenger who spoke with Huáscar witnessed that he raised his arms high to indicate his defeat. He finds this gesture similar to the one used by Abraham.

(6) Indians, like Jews, call each other "brother," even when they are not.

(7) Indian priests anoint themselves with *Ulli,* an oil substitute.

(8) There is a connection between the Jewish and Indian customs of taking the dead to their native land, where they are buried in mounds.

FRAY FERNANDO,
Lay Brother of the Convent
of La Merced

# CULTURAL NEWS

### AL JOLSON IN LIMA

When it was announced that the film "The Singing Fool," with Al Jolson in the title role, would be shown in this city, many members mistook this movie for another, already exhibited in several South American countries, in which Al Jolson sings several Jewish songs.

For this reason, we saw a large number of Jews at the film's debut at the "Iris." Though disappointed when they realized that Jolson would not ʂing any Jewish songs, they all enjoyed what turned out to be an intensely dramatic movie.

---

# ANNOUNCEMENT

### FELLOW JEWS!

Give your financial support to our fellow Jews in Palestine. There, in the Holy Land, is the man of tomorrow. There, close to the earth, are the ideals of the "new man," the man who leaves behind comfort, wealth, and position to till the land that the Jewish community is reconquering for its people.

—THE EDITORS

# Chronicles: 1935

The first performance of the work "Der Dorf's Yung," by L. Kobrin, takes place in the Bolognesi Theater. Messrs. Alberto Saiman, Marcos Kuperman, Boris Rostein, and Jacobo Fishman, and Miss Victoria Weinstein, all play their roles very well and are rewarded with the applause of the public.

When Jacobo Lerner reads the article in *Jewish Soul* on the similarities between Indian and Jewish cultures, he remembers the day when Rabbi Schneider told him that in 1921, while still living in Colombia, he took a trip through the jungle to visit the Jewish community in Iquitos. He got lost, and had he not been helped by a tribe of extremely civilized Indians, he would still be wandering in the Peruvian jungle.

The rabbi had been found by the Iquitos and had been taken to live with them for a time. What was most astounding is that he spoke to them in Hebrew and was perfectly understood.

Rabbi Schneider also told Jacobo that these Indians had received him in a totally different manner than they used to receive the missionaries who from time to time traveled through that region. The latter were usually slain, but he was received with the finest hospitality. He thought that perhaps, during Colonial times, rabbis might have traveled through on their way from Lima, and having found the tribe, taught them Hebrew. Only this could explain why they understood what he said, why their ceremonies were so similar to those of the Jews, and why the old man in charge of them was known as "raba."

Remembering these words of Rabbi Schneider's, Jacobo Lerner feels a very intense desire to leave Lima and disappear without a trace. He thinks that neither the affection he feels for his sister-in-law, nor his relationship with doña Juana, nor the satisfactory economic situation in which he finds himself have been enough to give meaning to his life.


The movie "The Jazz Singer," starring Al Jolson, that contains many scenes of Jewish life, finally arrives in Lima. The work deals with the conflict between two cultures, and in addition to scenes familiar to every Jew, it has moments of extreme dramatic tension. It is interesting to note the coincidence that this film, whose principal scene takes place during Yom Kippur, is shown during Rosh Hashana, a few days before the aforementioned festival.


On the night of October 11th, Doctor Bernardo Rabinowitz shows up at the house of Jacobo Lerner to tell him that he, Jacobo, is going to die. He tells this news without preparation, brusquely, as if it were a secret that he could no longer keep to himself. Jacobo Lerner receives the news as if it concerned someone else, someone that he hardly knows.


On the 10th of December there is an evening of poetry and music at the Hall of the Hebrew Union. The program is as follows:

Mr. Menahem Shapiro recites some poems of A. Reysen, dedicating them to don Moisés Lerner; Miss de Kristal, Miss Clara Abeler, and Miss Raquel Cogan declaim "The Three Ladies Sewing," by I. L. Peretz; Mr. Isaac Rostein, accompanied at the piano by Miss Nina Antonoff, sings "Eli, Eli," followed by an aria from "Faust."

At the conclusion of the program there is a dance that continues until late into the night.


# DREAMED BY JACOBO LERNER
## ON THE NIGHT OF OCTOBER 11, 1935


slow     procession   down-street   bells     pealing   smoke    up-
spiraling   men wrapped in black capes   braziers   red-hot coals
   incense   hooded monks   wooden cross   back of man stripped to waist   arrows                      lying on bed of
roses   rabbi water   Indians   water   open window   woman looking   woman bare-breasted   laughing   looking   do not laugh
   please   do not laugh   there are people waiting in the church
                           steeple     blind   watch-
man   signaling   OPEN DOOR               philacteries   talis
taking me   taking me taking   me   taking me   taking me   taking
me           round           table   white               tablecloth
   food                   Moisés thank you thank you
thank   you        invitation   funeral   Sara   serve   the   water
Sara                 Sara                           rabbi
serve the water rabbi   all trains have stopped in the middle of the
way   Sara's dress is threadbare               YOU MUST
HELP   YOUR   BROTHER   rabbi   there   is   blood   on   my
forehead   handkerchief   blood   too late too late too late   this
man is dead   Moisés puts gun away   rabbi just arrived   jungle
water looking for water        SARA   give the rabbi some
water       voices       calling voices out all out       but not the
dead man   asleep on the table blood flowing
white tablecloth

JACOBO YOU MUST HELP DANIEL

who throws revolver out the window
woman    looking    crying I    want    to    see    my    son
CLOSE    THE    WINDOW
darkness    stairs    ropes    bells pealing
cavern    RABBI
"after death we descend to a subterranean place"

back    door    monks
hooded    candles

"place of darkness for sinners and for
saints"    small white casket    shoulders    placed at red hot
cross    "from where there is no return"    circle of hooded monks
bowed heads    hands crossed all    around
the    casket    "saints and sinners alike"

rabbi    Hebrew    prayers    cas-
ket    Hebrew    "rest ye woeful one"    León FATHER
CHIRINOS    knees    prayers    "souls    that    are
shadows"    closer    come closer    chills    runrun-
runrunrunrun    run    run    run    run    run    run
flee    drag    your-
self    out    PLEASE DO    NOT DRAG ME    Moisés
"existence there is pale"    open the casket go on
open    "God there has his    hand    on    all    souls"    open
the    casket    son bed roses
ashes and dust son

# XIX

## *Samuel Edelman: Chepén, December 19, 1935*

EVERYTHING IS finished. When I arrived in Chepén this morning it seemed as if things were starting again, but everything is over . . . Felisa was right. Why did I come to this town? Didn't I know what was going to happen? I came for nothing. Nothing good could have been expected from this town, but man, man thinks all roads are good. . . . I had hoped to do something for Jacobo now that he is dying. I thought perhaps there would be a miracle: I would find Efraín in good health and take him to his side. . . .

Tomorrow I leave for Lima. There is no time to lose. I have to tell him the news of his son. God, I have no strength to see another man die! Deaths, deaths, nothing but deaths. I don't want to go to Lima. What am I going to tell him? I found your son; he is like León; there is no hope? It would be better if he were already dead, at least he would have one less suffering to go through. Why more pain?

Let the past be buried in this town. Time has taken care of everything. Everything is torn and worn. Nothing can be recovered. All illusions have long gone. Why should I tell him about Efraín? Why should I go to Lima? Wouldn't it be better to stay in Chiclayo and forget about Jacobo once and for all? I could open a store and stay there to live with Felisa and my children. I am tired of traveling . . . always the same strange faces everywhere, always the nights alone in cold hotel rooms. It is time to stay in Chiclayo. I have nothing to do in Lima. In this town, everything is finished.

But when man thinks he is finished then everything begins anew, says the Talmud. . . .

If I go to Lima I am not going to tell Jacobo the truth. I'll tell him only that they didn't want to give me the boy, but that he is growing strong and healthy as he should be.

Everything is finished now. It is better if I forget this village forever. There are bad memories everywhere. Everything makes me think of León. I think I see him everywhere, like a shadow . . . here in the hotel room I think he is looking at me from the dark corners, saying nothing, eyes lit by a strange flame. I remember the night he died. I hear him calling out for the rabbi, screaming. He knew he was going to die. Call the rabbi, call the rabbi, he told me, twisting in his bed like a snake, holding his stomach. Then he was quiet. I thought the danger had passed. He was smiling. He remembered his village. Then again the screaming, again. Then a long silence . . .

His face was twisted. His body was bent like a fetus. I don't know how the blind woman knew he had died, but she came in and straightened him up, crossing his hands on his chest. But I didn't dare touch him.

She didn't cry a single tear. She went back to her room. I never saw her again until the time when we put the casket on the bus. How were we to know it would get lost?

I spent days looking for it, from town to town. There was no casket anywhere. And who knows where it is now? When I told Jacobo he said he was sure they had buried him and had put a cross on his tomb. I couldn't sleep with that thought. When I slept I dreamed of León's death. I saw him drowned in the river and burned in fire. I saw him die in a thousand manners. And every time there was a cross there.

How strange it is to see this town without León. I remember him walking down the street, or sitting behind the counter in his store. The town is empty without him. The store is still closed. No one has reopened it. People must be afraid of the place. Maybe Felisa is right. They killed León. The best thing I can do is leave the hotel very early in the morning, so that no one will see me in the streets. I will wait only until the sun comes up.

It must be three in the morning already. Time doesn't seem to move in this town. Father Chirinos blamed León for everything. He said the Mayor died in the Trujillo jail. Also that Jacobo brought ruin to the Wilsons. He was a punishment from God. . . .

I am afraid to stay in this town. Everything here goes from bad to worse. If I could only sleep for a little while. But how am I going to sleep in this town? They are capable of coming into the room and stealing everything I have.

Felisa was so right. If only I had paid attention to her. This morning when I went to Wilson's house I thought the people were going to jump on me. Thank God tomorrow I leave Chepén. Since I arrived here everything has been like a nightmare. Why revive the past? Why remember things that make one's heart hurt?

It's the same fear I had every time I came to see León. I thought they would make me pay for what Jacobo had done. What fault was it of mine? They were following me down the street when I went to see old man Wilson this morning. They stared at me from head to foot. People opened their windows to watch me go by.

When I went into the Wilson's house it was like going into a graveyard. Everything was dark as if it were beneath the earth. I wanted to leave right then, even without seeing the boy.

I told old man Wilson: I have come to take the boy to his father.

He took me to a room without furniture, and there, in a corner, was Efraín, kneeling down, face to the wall. When he turned around he had a strange smile on his lips. Worse than the last time I had seen him! His clothes were dirty. He had the smell of death. I couldn't take him to Lima.

I told old man Wilson: I can't take him like this. And he cursed Jacobo. Said he didn't want the boy in his house. Told me to take him to his father.

His father is dying, I told him.

Then you take him, he screamed. You take him. How

could I take him, sick like that, to live with Felisa and my children? Then Efraín's mother began laughing and laughing. She sat on the bed combing her hair. She looked like an old woman, with her face full of wrinkles, speaking of things I didn't understand.

And then I went back to Efraín, kneeling in the corner. His eyes were lost, God knows where. What am I going to tell Jacobo, I thought.

It would be so much better if Jacobo had already died.

Then Father Chirinos came, and he didn't even look at Efraín. Jacobo's death is the punishment of God, he said. His death is the punishment of God, just like León's was. He had brought a curse to Chepén. Everything started happening when León arrived. Even the earthquake they had had a few years before was the fault of León. . . .

Bad times for the Jews. We do no harm to anybody. They are all lies. Even the papers are full of slander every day. Maybe León's prophecies, maybe? . . .

I said nothing to the priest. I wasn't going to fight with him after what had happened. After the blind woman died, they burned León's house. Nothing is left of León in this town, only bad memories, everywhere bad memories. He was mad to stay and live in Chepén. Jacobo was right in going to Lima. Am I going to be in time, before he dies? What am I going to tell him about Efraín? I can't tell him the truth. It would be like killing him. You can't tell a father something like that about his son. The boy is not well, Jacobo. It would be better if he stayed with his mother, Jacobo.

Felisa was right. It was a waste of time to come to Chepén. And if I go to Lima and everything is finished, that too will be a waste of time  But if I don't go, who is going to take care of Jacobo's burial? Moisés is not going to do anything for his brother. They are just going to leave him there, in his house, and no one else will know he died. It is my duty as a Jew to go and bury him. After what happened to Leon's body, I can't take a chance with Jacobo. I am going to go and bury him like a Jew, the way it should be.

I'll tell him to forget Efraín. Jacobo, I'll tell him, it's better to forget that town once and for all.

# GUIDE FOR THE PERFECT
## JEWISH GENTLEMAN

—Pay attention to the lessons of God and do not shun His punishment. He punishes whom He loves and tries whom He prefers.

—Be a citizen of the world. Be a man and a Jew, but be a Jew with pride.

—Do not rejoice in your enemy's ruin; keep happiness from your heart as he falls. If God sees it and He is displeased, He will stay His anger from His head.

—If your enemy is hungry, feed him; if he is thirsty, give him to drink. That way you pour burning coals on his head.

—Let the doors of your house be open. Consider the poor as members of your family.

—Do not live from your dreams. Dreams have no importance at all.

—To live without marriage is as grave a sin as murder.

—Correct your son and he will give you happiness. He will be the joy of your soul.

—He who does not attempt to learn does not deserve to live.

—The wise man follows a path upward, away from the *seol.*

—Follow the example of God, and like Him, be modest.

—Do not count on tomorrow, because you don't know what it might bring. The steps of man are guided by God. What can man know about his own destiny?

—Know what has happened and what is to happen. Interpret all signs. Watch the change of seasons and the passing of time.

—Never ask why times past were better. You will never know how to ask this question wisely.

—Keep away from evil company for two reasons: to protect yourself from their evil and to avoid learning from them.

—Be just. Justice is the way of the good man. The way of the evil man leads to death.

—Keep the Law. No one tries to deceive at the hour of his death.

—Renew in yourself the miracle of a new Christ, and carry your cross with dignity.

# EDITORIAL

It is painful, but it must be said, and clearly: our economic practices are what cause, to a large extent, the atmosphere of hostility against us. More and more often articles appear in the press in which voices are raised against us. This is only a symptom of far graver things to come if we don't know how to prevent them. . . .

There are two factors that contribute to the animosity that exists against the Jewish community: the lack of industrial development in the country, and the excessive spirit of philanthropy and mutual protection that has developed among us Jews.

It is a fact that Jewish merchants, driven by their intense desire to protect each other, allow all those who have just arrived in the country to join their ranks. It is a fact, as well, that in their desire for profits, wholesalers have encouraged Jews to become peddlers rather than practice whatever trade or profession they had in their country of origin.

If this were not so, we would have today a great number of Jewish artisans, well specialized, with every prospect of success, offering to the community a great economic advantage. What we must do is encourage the new immigrant to engage in physical labor and to stop him, by no matter what means, from becoming a traveling salesman.

We must awaken in those Jews who are currently commercial travelers the desire to close their ranks to newcomers. Only in this way can we demonstrate with facts that the word "Jew" is not synonymous with "peddler."

—THE EDITORS

# ATTENTION!

ALL THOSE WHO SEE US, THE JEWS, AS MERE MEMBERS OF A
RELIGIOUS GROUP ARE IN GREAT ERROR. WE ARE A NATION, WITH
ALL THE RIGHTS OF A NATION. MANY OF US ARE ENEMIES OF
RELIGION AND OF RELIGIOUS PRACTICE.

---

# THE YELLOW CARD

THE MOST GRIPPING DRAMA OF THE YEAR
The story of MARYA KALISH

a young Jewish girl pursued
by an emissary of the Czar

DO NOT MISS THIS GREAT THEATRICAL EVENT

Thursday, December 8

MUNICIPAL THEATER

---

BECOME A PERUVIAN CITIZEN!

# JEWS, ATTENTION!

We know there are members of the community in Lima and other cities on the coast who buy from wholesalers whose proprietors or managers engage in open Nazi and anti-Semitic activities.

FELLOW JEW: You are making a grave mistake in aiding the enrichment of these people with your purchases. You must repudiate them, and it is your duty to do so!

NOT ONE MORE CENT TO THE ENEMY!

THE BLOOD OF YOUR SACRIFICED BROTHERS DEMANDS IT!

—THE EDITORS

# XX

HE RAISED himself on the bed as if he were a bundle, rubbed his eyes, and looked into the mirror. Jacobo Lerner had just passed his forty-second birthday when he was told he was going to die. After he had heard the news he spent a full week locked up in his house, opening his door to no one, not even to doña Juana Paredes who, unaware of what was happening, had come to see him three times.

When he finally decided to leave the house, he went to the post office, a couple of blocks away, to send a letter to Samuel Edelman. Since he did not know Edelman's whereabouts, he addressed the letter to the closed store of León Mitrani, trusting that some neighbor would give it to Edelman as he passed through the town.

As soon as he had posted the letter, Jacobo returned home where, from that moment on, he lived the life of a complete recluse. With the exception of the maid who took care of the house and of Doctor Rabinowitz who came to see him twice a week, Jacobo kept away from friends and relatives, holding onto the hope that through perfect rest he would soon be well.

Only now, after two months, lying like a fetus between the sheets, rising and looking at himself in the mirror, seeing his eyes bleary for lack of sleep, his skin turned to the color of dirty parchment, Jacobo began to believe the fact of his own imminent death.

He found it very difficult to recognize the image in the mirror. At first he thought that the being who looked at him almost mockingly from the silvery surface was his brother Moisés, who had come to take away the portrait of their parents. Then he imagined the thin figure with the dark circles under the eyes was old man Wilson who, after ten years, had sneaked into the room to bring him to account. Finally, as if a mysterious hand shuffled faded engravings in front of his eyes, he saw his father's face, that of Rabbi Finkelstein, that of the priest in Chepén, that of Bertila, and that of León Mitrani.

He looked at himself in the mirror for a few seconds, forced a smile, and let himself drop back down onto the pillow. As if through a veil, he saw the body of León Mitrani, the bloody face of Daniel Abramowitz on the night they took him to the hospital, the body of Marcos Geller in the Cemetery of the Angels, and the fragmented image of his son praying on his knees in the church of Chepén.

When this last vision came, Jacobo covered his face with his hands and, mechanically, remembered the time in 1932 when Bertila had come to his house to offer him his son. He had thrown her out into the street after insulting her and telling her that he wasn't even sure Efraín was his son; he thought he had done well to escape from Chepén in time. He imagined if he had stayed in that village he would have been, at that very minute, sitting behind a counter like León Mitrani, with dust in his eyebrows and his eyes lost in the distance like an old lame animal.

Exhausted by the tangle of memories, Jacobo Lerner sank his head in the pillow, and suddenly, as if a dream had become a reality, he saw himself a well man, healthy and happy, being visited by friends and family. He saw himself wealthy, living a long life in which he fathered numerous children, as if he were one of the patriarchs in Genesis.

When he opened his eyes he examined, astounded, the loneliness of his room. After a long while, his thoughts tried in vain to recapture some happy experience in the past. He held his breath to find out how it would feel to be dead, but his eyes continued to perceive what was around him: the slight waving of the curtains, dust shot through by a shaft of sunlight, a few gray clouds escaping from the frame of the window. He closed his eyes. He felt faint. He believed they were lowering him into the grave, and he saw it was to the right of León Mitrani. As if coming from a very distant place he heard the voice of Rabbi Schneider: "All, evil and good, go down to the *seol* where they lead a consciousless existence akin to sleep." Then he saw how they threw the first shovelful of earth on him, while Father Chirinos, standing by the side of the grave, made the sign of the cross.

When he opened his eyes again it seemed to him that the room was darker. He felt a slight chill running up and down his back. He knew it was going to rain all night and instinctively he put his arms under the blanket.

## THE JEWS AND THE INQUISITION

(Exclusive for *Jewish Soul*)

The means of torture used during the Inquisition are among the most terrifying ever used by man. We can rightfully say that we have no feelings if our nerves do not contract in horror when we only imagine the writhings of a body condemned to the flames.

Not a few Jews were condemned to this martyrdom in the pious and tranquil squares of our cities, in the name of a civilization and a crucifix.

FRAY FERNANDO,
Lay Brother of the Convent
of La Merced

---

## BOLOGNESI HALL

Wednesday, January 4th, 1936

EVENING PERFORMANCE: 9:30

Presents the great melodrama in 4 acts by

### JULIUS MAQUELSON

*WI IZ MAIN HEIM?*
(*Where Is My Home?*)

# POLICE DEPARTMENT

### ALIEN REGISTRATION

We remind all foreign residents of Lima and the Province of Callao that by the 30th of December they must register for the second trimester of this year as required by law.

Those who fail to do so will be liable to prosecution under the law.

—THE BUREAU CHIEF

---

# GRAND BALL!

On Thursday, December 31, to celebrate

### THE ARRIVAL OF 1936

Music for dancing will be provided by a renowned orchestra. There will be a buffet dinner, and a GRAND PRIZE to the lady who has received the greatest number of letters by AIR MAIL.

Time: 9:00

Every member of the community in Lima and cities along the shore is invited.

—THE COMMITTEE

# XXI

## *Efraín: Chepén,*
## *December 25, 1935*

THE SPIDER goes up and down, hanging on its thread. It is like spit, the thread. Little spider, where are you going? I'm not going to let you leave that corner because if you do you are going to go into your hole and leave me alone, like the others. What are you going to do in your hole? You are going to bump into things because it is very dark, and when you fall through down into the river you are going to drown because you don't know how to swim.

Where could everyone be? They always leave me all alone. Only Aunt Francisca comes to give me something to eat, and afterward she crosses my hands on my chest, as if I were dead, and prays three Our Fathers. I just look at her, without opening my mouth because it is full of food, and she screams at me. Don't look at me like that, like an ass, she screams, and I laugh to myself because her face gets all twisted up with anger.

Don't go into your hole, little spider. Here in the corner we are going to build a house big enough for both of us, out of your threads. We will hide from everyone and they'll never find us again. If Ricardo tries to get in we'll spit at him and his face will rot like a dead man's. Two green worms will come out of his eyes and he will not be able to cry.

Grandmother says that in this corner there are suffering spirits. Are you afraid of spirits, little spider? I'm not afraid of them. If any spirit shows up I'll open my mouth and swallow it. How would it feel to have a spirit inside of me? Grandmother says a wandering soul got inside the Chang woman, and she died because she had a spirit inside her chest. That's when the whole town burned up after lightning hit Father Chirinos. He stood like a tree in the middle of the street afterward, white and dry as a bone, without any leaves. Then everyone left and I stayed all alone in the town. Only Mr. Mitrani stayed, sitting in his store. The fire didn't even touch it. His wife burned up in his house, though. Grandfather said she was the one who had lit the first match. When all the houses were burned up, and the ashes were mixed with the dirty rain that fell, Grandfather returned with the whole family and asked me how it was that I was still alive.

Get out of the hole at once! Don't you see the house is ready? We will let my father in because he has no house. He only has a store, because his house burned up as well. They couldn't find his bones hanging from the ceiling in Doctor Meneses' office. I'm going to get them down and I'm going to bury them. I don't want them to get lost, the same as the scapulary that Grandmother gave me. I looked for it all over the house, even in Grandfather's trunk. Aunt Francisca is going to beat me.

If you want to we'll see each other in church, like last time. This time I'm going to talk to you. Father Chirinos said I shouldn't speak to you, so that you would walk by my side without recognizing me and go back to Lima, alone, without Mr. Mitrani, who stayed in his store. If a dark man dressed as a gypsy comes, little spider, you'll open the door for him and you'll let him in. But don't let in anyone else. Don't let Grandfather in, because he will cut your legs off with scissors, one by one, slowly and gently so that you don't feel anything, and once he has them he will glue them to the notebook to give to doña Angelita.

Have you seen my father, little spider? Tell me, what color are his eyes? Are they the color of the water in which the drunk drowned? Aunt Francisca doesn't remember his eyes. Where is Bertila, so that she can see his eyes? She is going to die from fright when she sees them.

How are you, Father? What do you look like? If you are like Mr. Mitrani then your eyelashes are curly and you can fly. Isn't it true that you can fly? Let's fly away and never return. Bertila is going to be very sad when she finds out you've been here while she was in Pacasmayo with Irma, so that she didn't see you.

But there is plenty of room in our house. If you come I'll give you my room, just for yourself, with the dolls that Iris gave me. Iris went with the nuns. Grandfather says she is going to live in a convent and she is going to marry Jesus Christ. Father Chirinos is going to give them his blessing. He doesn't bless me anymore, because he's afraid I'm going to eat him.

The dolls have no arms, Father. This one, with the red dress, has no head. She was walking around the house at night and the cat must have eaten her head, because there was a big red bloodstain on the floor, and he was licking it with his sticky tongue.

Bertila slit her wrists on purpose, to see me cry, and now she's gone.

Where did Bertila go, little spider? She left with the engineer who has a red scar, she went on his truck, down the big highway. She's not going to be able to come back to see my father. She's never going to come back. Grandmother says that it is because Irma died and Bertila has to stay in Pacasmayo forever, to take care of her daughters. The only one who takes care of me is Aunt Francisca, and she never takes me to her house anymore, or even to school, or to church. In church I could see Jesus Christ, who is Iris' husband, with his legs full of blood. She used to stroke my head, but she doesn't do that anymore, either. Doña Angelita sends me candy with Ricardo, but he doesn't get too close because Grandmother has told him that whatever I have is catching.

Let's go to sleep, here in the corner, little spider. Don't

come down into my mouth at night because I'll eat you. Aunt Francisca says if I go on playing with myself my mouth is going to fill up with sticky snot, and you are going to let yourself down from the ceiling, gently, and are going to shit in my mouth. But I'm not going to let you.

How is Father's mouth? I'm sure it must be very sticky from all the spiders that he eats. Do you like spiders, Father? If you like spiders I'm going to take you to the yard at night and I'm going to show you all the spiders I have there. They are going to be sleeping and dreaming of angels and are not even going to realize that we will be looking at them. They have big eyes, like balls of shiny glass. The biggest one is the grandmother. Her belly is so big she can hardly walk. She sits dreaming all day, with her head full of lice, and she doesn't even prepare dinner for the little spiders. The skinny one is the grandfather. He spends all the time digging a hole to keep his money in. No one goes in there, because it is very dark and it is very deep. Here is Bertila, all ready with her lipstick to go to Pacasmayo with the engineer. Beatriz wants to run away, but I'm going to put her back in her place right now. I won't let Zoila go out either. If she does, I am going to tell Aunt Francisca and she is going to strap her with her belt, the way Grandfather used to do to me when I went into his room.

Which one do you like best, Father? Why don't you like Bertila? Shall we let her go? It doesn't matter, anyway. She's gone already, and she's not going to come back. César is not going to come back either. Grandfather says the Colombians killed him in the war. They went into the town and broke open people's heads with their bayonets so that they were dripping blood. But then the Peruvians returned, and Beatriz was carried away by a captain on a white horse. Are you going to come in your car, Father? Yes. In a car. And you'll wake up the whole town with the horn.

We'll let Mr. Mitrani into our house, Father, because Mr. Mitrani is going to return from heaven, just like the spider, hanging from a thin thread. Is the thread made of gold? Grandfather says that in your house in Lima everything is made of gold that shines and shines so it is never dark, not even at night, and no one can have bad dreams. When you come are you going to take me away with all the spiders, so that you can eat them?

But he is not going to eat you, little spider, because I'm not going to give you to anyone. If you go away I am the only one who's going to be left here. Only you and I live in this house. Uncle Pedro died in the toilet. He farted, and then he died. All afternoon he sat in the outhouse and his ass was covered by red flies while he sat, as if he were sleeping. Aunt Francisca went to wipe him, but no matter how hard she tried, she couldn't wake him up. I'm sure he was dreaming of something very nice, because I don't like to wake up when I dream of things I like. That way I am with my father and nothing can separate us. Grandfather came and loaded Uncle Pedro onto his shoulders and brought him inside to put him on the bed. His thing was long, like a black snake. Aunt Francisca straightened his neck and shaved him, so that he looked younger. He didn't even look like a dead man anymore, because dead men are very dirty. Their fingernails grow and they turn yellow from clawing the earth.

They dressed him in one of Grandfather's old suits, with a white shirt and a red tie around his neck, choking him. The whole night he was in the living room, with candles all around, and he couldn't breathe. In the morning they buried him in the yard where the pigs are, and, you know what, little spider? They ate him, shoes and all.

Don't come too close to my mouth, little spider, because I'll eat you.

Father is not coming today because it is very late. When they close the drugstore Zoila will come and they will lay there on that bed as if they didn't see us here, little spider, and we will see everything they do to each other. He touches her and she wriggles under the sheets. One of these days she is going to die from the pain, but they just don't care that I am here and I see them and I get dizzy. Aunt Francisca says it must be something sent from heaven, but Father Chirinos says that I am crazy. We aren't going to let Father Chirinos in, Father, not even if he comes with the whole town, threatening to break down the door.

If a spirit gets inside my body I am going to die from dizziness, because there is no one home. Everyone has left so that you could come. Do you look a lot like Mr. Mitrani, Father? When you come in, leave your cane on that chair. Mr. Mitrani loved me a lot and called me son, because he didn't know that I am the son of the rock.

Don't be frightened, little spider. I'm not going to crush you so that all your blood oozes out.

Bertila tried to kill herself so that my father would come to see me, but he didn't. Another tall man came, with an old leather suitcase. They brought him to our corner, little spider, and Grandfather told him we were playing hide and seek.

I didn't see his face, but it must have been all dirty from eating spiders. Then he left with his suitcase and Grandfather went on damning his luck. What was he going to do with me, he said, now that Bertila doesn't even live in this house, and I am costing him an arm and a leg. Grandfather told me that you died, Father. But I don't believe it. Come see me, and we will go away together to live in Mr. Mitrani's house where Father Chirinos can't get us. If he does, he'll drag us out into the street where people will throw stones at us. I should not eat spiders, Aunt Francisca says. If I do, she says, I'm going to shit worms, and that is very disgusting.

Why did they bury Uncle Pedro out in the yard? He'll never come out again from the hole where they buried him, even if he keeps everyone up all night, scratching with his long nails.

If you go into your hole, little spider, I am going to give you a lemon drop so you'll come out quickly, and we will both drag ourselves through the town so that everyone can see us and die of fright. We'll go to Mr. Mitrani's store and we will see him because we are not afraid of him anymore. And we'll go to the house of the Mirandas and we will throw stones until we break all the windows so that they cut their arms on the broken glass. And we'll go to church and we will break all of Father Chirinos' saints so that he has to bury them next to Uncle Pedro and so that my father will be happy when he comes.

We are going to have an earthquake. Grandfather says that's what happened when Mr. Mitrani came to live in town.

185

Houses and trees flew through the air and the dead were thrown out of the graveyard.

Then we'll return home and we will go to sleep together, hugging. That's why I am going to cut your little legs off, and I squeeze your head with my fingers, and I tear it off, slowly, and I crunch your body so that you can't feel anything when I chew you. . . .